Learning to Learn Together

This book brings together a range of international studies to support the implementation of cooperative group work in the classroom. In spite of extensive research into the benefits of this approach, in many countries, it is not widely used, largely due to a lack of understanding of how to put this into practice in the classroom. Starting from an exploration of the theoretical perspectives that underpin this pedagogy, the challenges for including pupils with special educational needs and related status issues of pupils are explored. Amongst the themes explored are how creative approaches, such as storyline, support engagement particularly for second language learning; how working with young children using cooperative group work can develop writing skills; and how teachers can work together in an effective, collaborative, and sustained manner in a professional learning community. The final chapter provides a vivid example of one teacher's personal journal to develop her understanding of the power of cooperation in creating bridges to meaningful learning for all learners. This book was originally published as a special issue of *Education 3–13*.

Wendy Jolliffe is the Head of Teacher Education at the University of Hull, UK. She has worked as a national and local adviser for teacher training and literacy, and was the Deputy Head of a Primary school in Hull before moving into higher education. Her teaching and research interests have focused on the implementation of cooperative learning, which is the subject of her PhD. She has run professional development courses in the United Kingdom and overseas on this subject. She is the author of *Cooperative Learning in the Classroom: Putting It into Practice* (2007) and is a member of the Board of International Association for the Study of Cooperative Education.

Learning to Learn Together

Cooperation, theory, and practice

Edited by
Wendy Jolliffe

LONDON AND NEW YORK

First published 2016
by Routledge
2 Park Square, Milton Park, Abingdon, Oxon, OX14 4RN, UK

and by Routledge
711 Third Avenue, New York, NY 10017, USA

Routledge is an imprint of the Taylor & Francis Group, an informa business

© 2016 Association for the Study of Primary Education

All rights reserved. No part of this book may be reprinted or reproduced or utilised in any form or by any electronic, mechanical, or other means, now known or hereafter invented, including photocopying and recording, or in any information storage or retrieval system, without permission in writing from the publishers.

Trademark notice: Product or corporate names may be trademarks or registered trademarks, and are used only for identification and explanation without intent to infringe.

British Library Cataloguing in Publication Data
A catalogue record for this book is available from the British Library

ISBN 13: 978-1-138-66569-9

Typeset in TimesNewRomanPS
by diacriTech, Chennai

Publisher's Note
The publisher accepts responsibility for any inconsistencies that may have arisen during the conversion of this book from journal articles to book chapters, namely the possible inclusion of journal terminology.

Disclaimer
Every effort has been made to contact copyright holders for their permission to reprint material in this book. The publishers would be grateful to hear from any copyright holder who is not here acknowledged and will undertake to rectify any errors or omissions in future editions of this book.

Contents

Citation Information	vii
Notes on Contributors	ix
Foreword	xi
Mark Brundrett	
Introduction – Learning to learn together: cooperation, theory and practice	xiii
Wendy Jolliffe	

1. Cooperative learning in elementary schools   1
   Robert E. Slavin

2. The challenges of implementing group work in primary school classrooms
   and including pupils with special educational needs   11
   Ed Baines, Peter Blatchford and Rob Webster

3. Status problem and expectations of competence: a challenging path for teachers   26
   Isabella Pescarmona

4. The Storyline approach: promoting learning through cooperation in the second
   language classroom   36
   Sharon Ahlquist

5. How to integrate cooperative skills training into learning tasks: an illustration
   with young pupils' writing   51
   Katia Lehraus

6. Bridging the gap: teachers cooperating together to implement
   cooperative learning   66
   Wendy Jolliffe

7. Meaningful learning in the cooperative classroom   79
   Yael Sharan

Index   91

Citation Information

The chapters in this book were originally published in *Education 3–13*, volume 43, issue 1 (February 2015). When citing this material, please use the original page numbering for each article, as follows:

Chapter 1
Cooperative learning in elementary schools
Robert E. Slavin
Education 3–13, volume 43, issue 1 (February 2015) pp. 5–14

Chapter 2
The challenges of implementing group work in primary school classrooms and including pupils with special educational needs
Ed Baines, Peter Blatchford and Rob Webster
Education 3–13, volume 43, issue 1 (February 2015) pp. 15–29

Chapter 3
Status problem and expectations of competence: a challenging path for teachers
Isabella Pescarmona
Education 3–13, volume 43, issue 1 (February 2015) pp. 30–39

Chapter 4
The Storyline approach: promoting learning through cooperation in the second language classroom
Sharon Ahlquist
Education 3–13, volume 43, issue 1 (February 2015) pp. 40–54

Chapter 5
How to integrate cooperative skills training into learning tasks: an illustration with young pupils' writing
Katia Lehraus
Education 3–13, volume 43, issue 1 (February 2015) pp. 55–69

Chapter 6
Bridging the gap: teachers cooperating together to implement cooperative learning
Wendy Jolliffe
Education 3–13, volume 43, issue 1 (February 2015) pp. 70–82

CITATION INFORMATION

Chapter 7
Meaningful learning in the cooperative classroom
Yael Sharan
Education 3–13, volume 43, issue 1 (February 2015) pp. 83–94

For any permission-related enquiries please visit:
http://www.tandfonline.com/page/help/permissions

Notes on Contributors

Sharon Ahlquist is a Senior Lecturer in TESOL and Applied Linguistics at the Högskolan Kristianstad, Sweden. Her interests lie in teaching and learning of English as a second language. Within this, her main focus is the storyline approach to facilitating the learning of English.

Ed Baines is a Senior Lecturer in Psychology of Education at the Institute of Education, UCL, London, UK. He is involved in a number of research projects, focusing on teaching, learning, and group work in classrooms, peer relations, friendships and social networks in schools, and peer interaction and dialogue. He is the author of *The Child at School: Interactions with Peers and Teachers* (with Anthony Pellegrini and Peter Blatchford, 2nd ed., 2015).

Peter Blatchford is a Professor of Psychology and Education at the Institute of Education, UCL, London, UK. His main area of interest is social developmental processes in school settings, and his recent research has included class size differences, the impact of teaching assistants, group work in classrooms, and social life in schools. He is the author of *The Child at School: Interactions with Peers and Teachers* (with Anthony Pellegrini and Ed Baines, 2nd ed., 2015).

Wendy Jolliffe is the Head of Teacher Education at the University of Hull, UK. She has worked as a national and local adviser for teacher training and literacy, and was the Deputy Head of a Primary school in Hull before moving into higher education. Her teaching and research interests have focused on the implementation of cooperative learning, which is the subject of her PhD. She has run professional development courses in the United Kingdom and overseas on this subject. She is the author of *Cooperative Learning in the Classroom: Putting It into Practice* (2007) and is a member of the Board of International Association for the Study of Cooperative Education.

Katia Lehraus is a Lecturer in the Faculty of Psychology and Educational Sciences at the University of Geneva, Switzerland. Her interests include cooperative learning, social interactions between students in learning situations, and training strategies for teachers. She is the editor of *Towards Learning in Cooperation: Meetings and Opportunities* (with Rouiller, 2008).

Isabella Pescarmona is an Adjunct Professor in the Department of Philosophy and Educational Sciences at the University of Turin, Italy. She is interested in cultural anthropology, comparative education, and teaching methods. Her work has appeared in *Education 3–13, Intercultural Education,* and the *International Journal of Pedagogies and Learning.*

NOTES ON CONTRIBUTORS

Yael Sharan has over thirty years of experience in developing, training and writing about cooperative learning and group investigation. She is the author of *Expanding Cooperative Learning through Group Investigation* (1992) and is an expert in adapting cooperative learning for diverse groups. She is a board member of the International Association for the Study of Cooperation in Education and a member of the Association for Intercultural Education.

Robert E. Slavin is the Professor and Director of the Center for Research and Reform in Education at Johns Hopkins University, Baltimore, MD, USA. He has written on topics including cooperative learning, comprehensive school reform, ability grouping, school and classroom organization, desegregation, mainstreaming, research review, and evidence-based reform. He is the author of *Educational Psychology: Theory into Practice* (11th ed., 2015).

Rob Webster is a Research Officer in the Department of Psychology and Human Development at the Institute of Education, UCL, London, UK. He leads the 'SEN in Secondary Education' study, which focuses on the educational experiences of students with high-level SEN. He also leads the programme for 'Maximising the Impact of Teaching Assistants'.

Foreword

This text springs out of a special issue of *Education 3–13: International Journal of Primary, Elementary and Early Years Education*. The journal was first published in 1973 and so, at the time of writing, is in its forty-third year of production. It is now published six times a year and is read not only in England and the wider UK, but is also distributed to academic institutions in many countries around the world in hard copy and electronic versions. It also enjoys an amazing success online with well over 100,000 articles downloaded every year.

During its more than forty years of existence, the journal has contributed positively to the complex and sometimes confusing discourse on how to educate children best from pre-school until the early years of secondary education. Throughout its history, *Education 3–13* has stood as one of the few journals dedicated to the work of teachers and other professional groups working with children in pre-school, primary, and middle schools. This makes it an unusual and important journal since it focuses on the one phase of schooling that is ubiquitous across all nations. Every issue of the journal is now available electronically in the archive on the journal website, www.tandfonline.com/toc/rett20/current.

Education 3–13 is owned by the Association for the Study of Primary Education (ASPE), which was founded on the core purpose of advancing the cause of primary education and on supporting those most directly involved through professional discourse, practice, and study. ASPE holds conferences and seminars on primary education and is often consulted about proposed changes to primary education that will be of interest to all members of the constituencies it seeks to represent. The journal attempts to reflect the purposes of the association and there is a close relationship between *Education 3–13* and ASPE with many of the members of the Association's Executive Committee taking key roles with the journal. Anyone who is interested in the journal, or in primary education more generally, is encouraged to explore the work of the association. More can be found out about ASPE, including how to become a member, on the ASPE website at www.aspe-uk.eu.

Both the editorial board of *Education 3–13* and the Executive Committee of ASPE were delighted when they were approached by Professor Wendy Jolliffe, who proposed to guest edit a special issue on the important topic of cooperative learning. What emerged was an outstanding special issue entitled 'Learning to learn together: cooperation theory and practice' (Volume 43, Number 1, 2015), which contained contributions from some of the most important scholars in the field. The special issue and this text offer a strong analytical framework for the successful implementation of cooperative approaches that should be of profound interest to teachers, teacher educators, and policy makers.

FOREWORD

Education 3–13 owes a great debt to the guest editors who give so willingly of their precious time to carry out the complex task of developing a proposal and then coordinating the writing, collation, and submission of a full journal issue. The debt is all the greater when a group of leading academics from different nations are brought together to share their research on an important topic of great contemporary interest and importance. Both the board of the journal and the Executive Committee of ASPE wish to express their profound thanks to Professor Jolliffe and her colleagues.

Professor Mark Brundrett
Editor, *Education 3–13: International Journal of Primary, Elementary and Early Years Education*

Introduction – Learning to learn together: cooperation, theory and practice

Wendy Jolliffe

This book brings together a range of studies to enhance understanding of cooperative group work in the classroom. This is a timely moment to revisit the extensively documented research benefits of this pedagogy and also to examine its manifestations across a range of countries and cultures. In England, a new National Curriculum came into force in 2014, and evidence shows that excellent teaching is the most powerful means of improving achievement (Barber and Mourshed, 2007; Hattie, 2009; OECD, 2005). Thus, what teachers actually do—their pedagogy—is firmly on the agenda, and yet as Alexander (2004, 2008) and Pollard (2010) argue, it is a much neglected, and often misunderstood, topic in England. The extensive ten-year ESRC 'Teaching Learning and Research Programme' (TLRP, 2007) culminated in a set of ten principles for effective pedagogy. This includes promoting learning as a social activity where learners should be encouraged to work with others, to share ideas and to build knowledge together. In spite of such research, its impact on practice in classrooms appears to be limited. The previous Secretary of State for Education, Michael Gove, declared that 'teaching is a craft and it is best learnt as an apprentice observing a master craftsman or woman' (DfE, 2010). If this is the case, developing a deep understanding of research into effective pedagogy has little place for teachers. This collection of papers argues to the contrary that the greater the understanding by teachers on how to ensure that classrooms provide opportunities for deep learning for all, through pupils working together cooperatively, the more effective learning will be.

This book brings together works from those who are eminent in the field, some of whom are seen as founding figures with extensive research spanning several decades, such as Robert Slavin and Yael Sharan. Providing a rich range of examples of research into practice from different contexts, it demonstrates not only why cooperative group work is successful in promoting education for all children, but also, perhaps more importantly, how this can be implemented in different contexts. However, it is not a 'quick fix' to school improvement. Implementation requires an in-depth understanding of why this approach works, as well as ongoing development of the skills required by pupils and teachers equally, using it effectively.

Different perspectives on cooperative learning (CL) are brought together in this book. Terms such as collaborative or cooperative learning are used as well as group work. This has previously often led to confusion. One of the underlying differences between the terms relates to two different epistemological perspectives. CL has evolved from the work of Lewin (1948) centered on group dynamics and further developed by the work of social psychologists, such as Johnson and Johnson (1975, 1990), Schmuck and Schmuck (2001), and Sharan (1990), into a theory of social interdependence. Collaborative learning's roots lie in constructivism (Kelly, 1955; Vygotsky, 1978; Rorty, 1979) and the work of Britton (1970), who supported the notion of creating a community of learners with a focus on dialogue to support learning

INTRODUCTION

and emphasising personal responsibility. Collaborative learning broadly rejects the structure and, as Panitz (n.d.) argues, it is a philosophy of interaction. In contrast, CL focuses on group interaction by considering group dynamics. This has led to the identification of the factors that are crucial in effective CL. According to Johnson and Johnson (2000), Slavin (1995), Kagan (1994), Cohen (1994), and Sharan and Sharan (1992, 1994), two aspects that are particularly essential are positive interdependence and individual accountability. Positive interdependence exists when individuals realise that they cannot succeed unless everyone in the group performs, and tasks are designed to facilitate this. Linked to this is the necessity for individual accountability, where each member of the group must be accountable for his or her share of the work. Other factors that are important include the group and individual reflection where groups monitor and assess their functioning and ensure the development of the necessary social and small group skills for groups to function successfully. Johnson and Johnson (1999, p. 73) summarise CL as 'the instructional use of small groups in which pupils work together to maximise their own and each other's learning'.

Extensive research has demonstrated the benefits of CL as supporting academic achievement, developing interpersonal skills, as well as heightening self-esteem and social competencies (Gillies, 2003; Jenkins et al., 2003; Johnson and Johnson, 1975, 1989; Jordan and Metais, 1997; Sharan, 1990; Slavin, 1995, 1996) and were also confirmed by a more recent meta-analysis (Kyndt et al., 2013). In spite of such findings, in England and elsewhere, CL is not widely used. Indeed, group work has been described as a 'neglected art' (Galton and Hargreaves, 2009, p. 1). One of the key reasons for this, as identified by Kutnick (2015), is that it requires pupils to have sufficient interpersonal, communication and support skills. Where clear training is given in these skills, as Gillies and Ashman's (1996) study showed, then pupils were consistently more cooperative and helpful to each other, used language which was more inclusive, and gave more explanations to assist each other. They also exercised more autonomy with their learning and obtained higher learning outcomes than untrained peers.

In addition to pupils who need to acquire the skills of working cooperatively, teachers too require support to be able to implement CL effectively in the classroom. A study by Lee (2015) examined a year-long teacher professional development programme in Singapore alongside the use of lesson study, and showed that the development of a collaborative learning culture amongst teachers was an instrument in implementing the use of CL. My research (2011, 2015) also identified the impact of collaboration across a network of schools in implementing CL as being crucial to success. Chapter 6 focuses on factors in effective professional development for teachers in CL, which emphasise the consideration of different phases of training. First, pre-training preparations, such as understanding theoretical perspectives of why it works and reconciling with personal beliefs. Second, training which models and provides experience of CL; and the third, and the most important, post-training support to sustain the use of CL in the classroom.

The two aspects of ensuring the development of pupils' skills of collaboration as well as teachers working collaboratively to sustain effective implementation are particularly crucial. As this book also demonstrates, providing examples from different contexts, cultures, and age groups helps in developing an understanding of the benefits of CL. It is expected that this will result in renewed interest in the potential of this pedagogy.

In the first chapter, Robert Slavin distils lessons from 30 years of research about CL and provides a summary of theoretical perspectives that underpin this pedagogy related to the elementary or primary school age. Slavin has written extensively about CL, documenting the benefits, and is regarded as one of its founding figures. In this chapter, he provides a theoretical model, which acknowledges the contributions of work from each of the major theoretical

xiv

INTRODUCTION

perspectives and the likely role that each plays. It is this synthesis that helps the reader understand that different theoretical standpoints are complementary rather than contradictory, and such standpoints explain the motivational advantages and cognitive processes that can be achieved through working together cooperatively. This forms a very helpful starting point for teachers wishing to use CL, supporting understanding of why it works. Slavin notes that whilst he provides a framework, 'there is still much more to be done' and 'research must continue to provide the practical, theoretical, and intellectual underpinnings to enable educators to achieve this potential' (page 8).

The next chapter looks at implementing group work in the primary classroom and particularly including pupils with special educational needs. This insightful study by Ed Baines, Peter Blatchford, and Rob Webster brings together two key areas that of inclusion of all learners and of issues of implementation. The findings from two complementary projects analyse the experiences of teachers implementing group work. Starting with the findings from the SPRinG (Social Pedagogic Research into Group-work), a five-year long ERSC-funded project in the United Kingdom (Baines et al., 2007; Kutnick et al., 2013), was developed to address the gap between the potential of group work to influence learning, on the one hand, and the limited use of group work in schools in the United Kingdom, on the other hand. They state in the end of award report (Blatchford et al., 2005, p. 33) that 'as far as we are aware this is the first study of group-work in the UK to show positive achievement gains in comparison to other forms of classroom pedagogy'. The chapter provides a summary of the positive findings of the study as well as the key principles and recommended practices, covering four main areas. These form a very useful guide for those wishing to effectively implement cooperative group work (see page 12).

Baines et al. (2007) identify some remaining challenges for teachers, particularly in relation to pupils with special educational needs. The second related project discussed, entitled *Making a Statement* (MAST), examined systematic observations and case studies of pupils with a 'statement' of special educational needs. Such pupils in England have undergone a statutory assessment process of their needs and then have a 'statement' setting out additional provision they are entitled to. In 2014, a new statutory code of practice in England replaced the requirement for a 'statement' with an Education, Health and Care Plan, in order to set out a more holistic attempt to meet a child's needs. The findings from this project provide a vivid picture of the isolation of many such children from peers in the classroom, often as a result of individual adult support from a teaching assistant and a lack of opportunities to work with peers. The case studies presented here show the potential for pupils with SEN to become more positively involved with peers. However, a lack of opportunities to do so is particularly worrying because many of these pupils have a real need to develop greater social skills. As Baines et al. (2007) conclude, 'peer learning approaches for all pupils need to be a central part of pedagogic practices that teachers utilise for enhancing learning in the 21st century' (page 23).

In Chapter 3, Isabella Pescarmona's study in Italy continues the theme of inclusion of all pupils in learning. It strongly reinforces the issues that may ensue from a lack of inclusive practices. She discusses teachers' conceptions of pupils' competence, which she terms as the 'status problem' and how the use of a CL approach, *complex instruction*, aimed to address this. Her ethnographic study is strongly based on the work of Cohen (1994) that defines the status problem as 'an agreed-upon social ranking where everyone feels it is better to have a high rank within the status order than a low rank' (Cohen, 1994, p. 27). This becomes a self-fulfilling prophecy by both pupils and teachers, aggravated by the common occurrence of some low-status pupils appearing passive or not engaged. From the premise of

xv

INTRODUCTION

'the more you talk, the more you learn, the less you talk, the less you learn' (page 27), based on a social-constructivist perspective of the importance of talk for learning, if 'low-status' pupils are not engaged in active discussion, their learning will suffer. As Pescarmona argues, if teachers do not make an effort to understand and act on conceptions of competence, the problem is exacerbated. She argues that using group work which emphasises the use of roles within groups, and which utilises pupils' differing skills, can change perceptions of pupil competence. This study aimed at investigating how six Italian primary school teachers interpreted the status problem; what criteria they used to define high- and low-status students; and how they implemented status treatment in classrooms. The results collected using an ethnographic approach demonstrated that such a process is complex. The study also provided a qualitative evaluation of the complex process of 'borrowing' ideas and practices from different contexts. In this case, the teachers did not just develop Cohen's status treatment as a 'ready-to-use' package. Instead, they mixed new ideas with their own educational perspectives. This is particularly important in considering the implementation of CL approaches in different cultural contexts and emphasises the importance of adapting practices rather than just 'adopting' them. The study included the teaching of social skills, referred to as 'skillbuilders' (Cohen, 1994), and the designing of group work with specific roles designated to different students, this is developed further to rotation of roles in groups in order to avoid continuing low status for some students. The study provides an insight into the difficulties teachers faced in assigning competencies to students and finding new strategies to cope up with status treatment successfully. As Pescarmona notes (page 34):

> the status problem is not something to be taken for granted, but is something to be questioned every time and evaluated in fieldwork. Its strength lies in the fact that is calls teachers and their expectations into question. Only by reflecting on this category will teachers be able to move closer to the goal of equity.

In another cultural context, in Sweden, Sharon Ahlquist discusses a project in Chapter 4 that harnesses the power of narrative using the Storyline approach. This originated in Scotland in the 1960s and developed further in the 1980s. A fictional world is created in the classroom, with learners working in small groups, taking on the role of characters in a story. It incorporates cooperative group work, including the important principles of positive interdependence and individual accountability, but its central focus is a developing narrative that pupils coconstruct. Starting with the developing of characters in the story, which students take on and keep for the duration of the topic, the story unfolds as groups work on key questions, which provide the impetus for the development of the story. For students aged 11–13 years, this approach proved highly motivational in engaging them in language learning and provided a meaningful context for speaking, reading, and writing in a second language which they had otherwise been reluctant to engage in. This type of cooperative group work has received little scholarly research to date. Ahlquist's study demonstrates the value of working in an imaginary setting, thereby diminishing the perceived risks of loss of face, particularly felt by adolescents, in speaking another language. This qualitative study used a range of sources of evidence to document the situation in these classrooms. Findings showed that students valued working together in groups and found learning in this way to be enjoyable. In particular, teachers reported that this stimulated their writing; the volume of which was unprecedented. What emerged was the sense of solidarity between students in groups, and they felt they were genuinely part of a 'family', even if this was fictional. A strong theme of inclusion yet again pervades this study, with teachers identifying how this helped in addressing the needs of the

xvi

INTRODUCTION

less able and the very able students. Using this approach, it was found that 'relationships build, both between the learners and the characters and between the learners themselves' (page 47). The impact of this affects the collaborative nature of learning in the classroom. As Ahlquist identifies, there is scope for further research in 'embedding the powerful tools of cooperative learning in a narrative framework' (page 47).

In Chapter 5, Katia Lehraus reports her research on the development of young children's writing in Switzerland, and examines how to integrate CL skills into learning tasks. By contributing to an area that has received considerably less attention and research, the use of CL with young children, this article discusses a research project with two primary school classes (ages 7–8 years) aimed at developing both cooperative and cognitive skills in writing. The results showed that young children were able to work cooperatively in pairs, without a teacher supporting them, on writing tasks. This therefore provides interesting reading for teachers who have previously often dismissed the use of cooperative group work with young children. It also demonstrates how children of this age can work independently of a teacher instead of relying on adult support, particularly in developing the complex cognitive processes involved in early writing. Developing such paired practices allows pupils to benefit from dialogue with peers and also enables the lightening of cognitive load required when writing.

The project consisted of two interventions aimed at developing both cooperative and writing skills in an interconnected way. Using the analysis of filmed episodes, pupils displayed high levels of on-task behaviour and paired support, resulting in often positive development of writing tasks. A key theme in this article is that the social and cooperative skills training programmes are often separated from learning situations in classrooms, leading to inconsistent outcomes; however, by embedding such skills in tasks, it can be more effective. As Lehraus summarises, 'learning to cooperate is necessary to be able to cooperate to learn' (page 62).

In Chapter 6, I aim to help bridge the gap between the potential of CL and its effective use in the classroom by drawing on literature into implementation together with empirical findings from a case study undertaken over five years into a network of schools in England (Jolliffe, 2011, 2015). A review of the literature identifies a number of key aspects in successful implementation. These begin with the pre-training preparation, starting with a thorough understanding of the theoretical and psychological perspectives that underpin learning and in particular the social–interdependence perspective which helps explain that each member of a group will cooperate for a goal which each one understands that everyone's contributions are required for the group to succeed. Teachers also need to examine their own preconceptions about learning and then reconcile these to a socio-constructivist view that values talk for learning. Learning about CL through experiencing it first-hand is a further crucial aspect (Brody, 2004), together with a phased approach to implementation which gradual builds confidence. Studies (Johnson and Johnson, 1994; Rolheiser and Stevahn, 1998; Schmuck, 1998) also show that it requires a collaborative and sustained approach to implementation, including coaching and co-teaching.

The case study cited demonstrates that teachers working together to develop CL can overcome the complexity of implementing this approach, particularly when supported by a professional learning community of facilitators, or in-house experts. The facilitators, working collaboratively across schools, supported each other and in turn provided invaluable coaching for teachers in each of their schools. When a group worked in this way across a network of schools, led by head teachers with a shared vision, the impact was visible. The study shows it takes time to build trust and effective cooperation between pupils in the classroom, between teachers in schools to support professional development, and between schools in networks and alliances. As interest grows internationally into teachers working together in professional

xvii

INTRODUCTION

learning communities, this article argues that this is not a 'quick fix' to school improvement. Such collaborative cultures offer the potential for 'transformative' professional development (Kennedy, 2005), and also bridge the gap between the benefits of CL and its effective use in the classroom.

In the final chapter, Yael Sharan presents a vivid picture of the impact of over 60 years' experience, documenting her personal journey to develop her understanding of the power of cooperation. How she learned to guide her students to use their own worlds as bridges to learning provides an example to others. For Sharan, it has become a life-long quest for ways to make learning meaningful to all learners in the complex reality of a classroom. The theme of inclusion related to the multi-cultural classroom pervades this account, like so many others in this special edition. The collaboration between student and teacher and between students in efforts to make learning meaningful creates an engaged classroom where students ask questions, share ideas and understanding, and construct meaningful knowledge. These are resounding features of CL methods. Sharan discusses the underlying 'theoretical mosaic that constitutes the CL approach' (page 85), as well as some of the implications for teaching, starting with the consideration of the role of questions which can have more than one answer; the structuring of learning in groups so that pupils can gain maximum benefit; and the carefully planned learning task. Not only teachers but also pupils require careful training to work in this way. Sharan's basic guidelines for implementing CL provide a clear path for teachers to try and emanate her journey to 'meaningful learning'.

This collection of studies provides a fascinating insight into the potential of CL in different countries, in different cultures, and with different ages. Whilst it requires sustained training of teachers and pupils to develop the necessary skills, it is hoped that the evidence cited here of effective and meaningful learning will stimulate a renewed interest and further research into CL as an effective pedagogy in the classroom. The twenty-first-century classroom needs to equip all pupils with skills for life: skills of communication, cooperation, and empathy. Working in this way has the potential to provide such a classroom.

References

Alexander, R. (2004). Still no pedagogy? Principle, pragmatism and compliance in primary education. *Cambridge Journal of Education 34*(1): 7–33.

Alexander, R. J. (2008). *Essays on Pedagogy*. London, UK: Routledge.

Baines, E., Blatchford, P., and Chowne, A. (2007). Improving the effectiveness of collaborative group-work in primary schools: effects on science attainment. ESRC Teaching and Learning Research Programme special issue of the *British Educational Research Journal 33*: 663–680.

Barber, M. and Mourshed, M. (2007). *How the World's Best Performing School Systems Come Out on Top*. London, UK: McKinsey & Company.

Blatchford, P., Galton, M., Kutnick, P., and Baines, E. (2005). *Improving the Effectiveness of Pupil Groups in Classrooms*, ESRC End of Research Report, ref: L139 25 1046. Available from: http://www.spring-project.org.uk (accessed 08.01.16).

Britton, J. (1970). *Language and Learning*. London, UK: Allen Lane.

Brody, C. M. (2004). The instructional design of cooperative learning for teacher education. In Cohen, E. G., Brody, C. M., and Sapon-Shevin, M. (Eds.), *Teaching Cooperative Learning: The Challenge for Teacher Education*. Albany, NY: State University of New York Press (pp. 185–194).

Cohen, E. (1994). *Designing Groupwork: Strategies for Heterogeneous Classrooms*. New York, NY: Teachers College Press.

DfE. (2010). *Michael Gove to the National College Annual Conference*, Birmingham (16 June 2010). Available from: https://www.gov.uk/government/speeches/michael-gove-to-the-national-college-annual-conference-birmingham (accessed 08.01.16).

INTRODUCTION

Galton, M. and Hargreaves, L. (2009). Group work: still a neglected art? *Cambridge Journal of Education* 39(1): 1–6.

Gillies, R. M. (2003). Structuring cooperative group work in classrooms. *International Journal of Educational Research 39*: 35–49.

Gillies, R. and Ashman A. (1996). Teaching collaborative skills to primary school children in classroom based work groups. *British Journal of Educational Psychology 65*: 211–25.

Hattie, J. (2009). *Visible Learning: A Synthesis of Over 800 Meta-Analyses Relating to Achievement.* London, UK: Routledge.

Jenkins, J., Antil, L., Wayne, S., and Vadasy, P. (2003). How cooperative learning works for special education and remedial students. *Exceptional Children 69*: 279–292.

Johnson, D. W. and Johnson, R. T. (1975). *Learning Together and Alone: Cooperative, Competitive and Individualistic Learning.* Needham Heights, MA: Allyn and Bacon.

Johnson, D. W. and Johnson, R. (1989). *Cooperation and Competition: Theory and Research.* Edina, MN: Interaction Book Company.

Johnson, D. W., Johnson, R. T., and Holubec, E. J. (1990). *Circles of Learning: Cooperation in the classroom* (3rd ed.). Edina, MN: Interaction Book Co.

Johnson, D. W. and Johnson, R. (1994). *Leading the Cooperative School* (2nd ed.). Edina, MN: Interaction Book Company.

Johnson, D. W. and Johnson, R.T. (1999). *Learning Together and Alone: Cooperative, Competitive and Individualistic Learning.* (5th ed.). Needham Heights, MA: Allyn and Bacon.

Johnson, D. W. and Johnson, F. P. (2000). *Joining Together: Group Theory and Group Skills* (6th ed.). Boston, MA: Allyn and Bacon.

Jolliffe, W. (2011). Co-operative learning: making it work in the classroom. *Journal of Co-operative Studies 44*(3): 31–42.

Jolliffe, W. (2015). Bridging the gap: teachers cooperating together to implement cooperative learning. *Education 3–13: International Journal of Primary, Elementary and Early Years Education 43*(1): 56–69.

Jordan, D. W. and Le Metais, J. (1997). Social skilling through cooperative learning. *Educational Research 39*: 3–21.

Kagan, S. (1994). *Cooperative Learning.* San Juan Capistrano, CA: Kagan Cooperative Learning.

Kelly, G. (1955). *A Theory of Personality.* New York, NY: Norton & Company.

Kennedy, A. (2005). Models of continuing professional development: a framework for analysis. *Journal of In-Service Education 31*(2): 235–250.

Kutnick, P. (2015). Developing effective group work in classrooms: a relational approach within a culturally appropriate pedagogy. In Gillies, R. M. (Ed.), *Collaborative Learning: Developments in Research and Practice.* New York, NY: Nova Science Publishers (pp. 117–139).

Kutnick, P., Blatchford P., Baines E., and Tolmie, A. (2013). *Effective Group-Work in Primary School Classrooms: The SPRinG Approach.* London, UK: Springer.

Kyndt, E., Raes, E., Lismont, B., Timmers, F., Cascallar, E., and Dochy, F. (2013). A meta-analysis of the effects of face-to-face cooperative learning. Do recent studies falsify or verify earlier findings? *Educational Research Review 10*: 133–149.

Lee, C. (2015). Developing communities of practice in cooperative learning (CoPCL) through lesson study. In Gillies, R. M. (Ed.), *Collaborative Learning: Developments in Research and Practice.* New York, NY: Nova Science Publishers (pp. 157–173).

Lewin, K. (1948). *Resolving Social Conflicts.* New York, NY: Harper.

OECD. (2005). *Teachers Matter: Attracting, Developing and Retaining Effective Teachers.* Paris, France: OECD.

Panitz, T. (n.d.). *Collaborative Versus Cooperative Learning—A Comparison of the Two Concepts Which Will Help Us Understand the Underlying Nature of Interactive Learning.* Available from: http://home.capecod.net/~tpanitz/tedsarticles/coopdefinition.htm (accessed 08.01.16).

Pollard, A. (Ed.). (2010). *Professionalism and Pedagogy: A Contemporary Opportunity A Commentary by TLRP and GTCE.* London, UK: TLRP.

Rolheiser, C. and Stevahn, L. (1998). The role of staff developers in promoting effective teacher decision-making. In Brody, C. M. and Davidson, N. (Eds.), *Professional Development for Cooperative Learning: Issues and Approaches.* Albany, NY: State University of New York Press (pp. 63–78).

INTRODUCTION

Rorty, R. (1979). *Philosophy and the Mirror of Nature*. Princeton, NJ: Princeton University Press.

Schmuck, R. (1998). Mutually-sustaining relationships between organisation development and coopera-tive learning. In Brody, C. M. and Davidson, N. (Eds.), *Professional Development for Cooperative Learning: Issues and Approaches*. Albany, NY: State University of New York (pp. 243–254).

Schmuck, R. A. and Schmuck, P. A. (2001). *Group Processes in the Classroom* (8th ed.). Boston, MA: MacGraw Hill.

Sharan, S. (1990). *Cooperative Learning: Theory and Research*. Westport, CN: Praeger.

Sharan, Y. and Sharan, S. (1992). *Expanding Cooperative Learning Through Group Investigation*. New York, NY: Teachers College Press.

Sharan, Y. and Sharan, S. (1994). Group investigation in the cooperative classroom. In Sharan, S. (Ed.), *Handbook of Cooperative Learning Methods*. Westport, CT: Praeger (pp. 97–114).

Slavin, R. (1995). *Cooperative Learning: Theory, Research, and Practice*. Boston, MA: Allyn and Bacon.

Slavin, R. (1996). *Education for All*. Lisse, The Netherlands: Swets & Zeitlinger.

Teaching and Learning Research Programme (TLRP). (2007). *Principles into Practice: A Teacher's Guide to Research Evidence on Teaching and Learning*. London, UK: TLRP.

Vygotsky, L. S. (1978). *Mind in Society: The Development of Higher Psychological Processes*. Cambridge, MA: Harvard University Press.

Cooperative learning in elementary schools[†]

Robert E. Slavin[a,b]

[a]*Center for Research and Reform in Education, Johns Hopkins University, Baltimore, MD, USA;*
[b]*Institute for Effective Education, University of York, York, UK*

> Cooperative learning refers to instructional methods in which students work in small groups to help each other learn. Although cooperative learning methods are used for different age groups, they are particularly popular in elementary (primary) schools. This article discusses methods and theoretical perspectives on cooperative learning for the elementary grades. The article acknowledges the contributions from each of the major theoretical perspectives and places them in a model that depicts the likely role each plays in cooperative learning outcomes. This work explores conditions under which each perspective may operate, and suggests further research needed to advance cooperative learning scholarship.

Cooperative learning refers to teaching methods in which students work together in small groups to help each other learn academic content. In one form or another, cooperative learning has been used and studied in every major subject, with students from pre-school to college, and in all types of schools. However, they have been particularly popular in the elementary grades, where greater flexibility in daily schedules makes it easier to do cooperative work.

There have been many studies of cooperative learning focusing on a wide variety of outcomes, including academic achievement in many subjects, second language learning, attendance, behaviour, intergroup relations, social cohesion, acceptance of classmates with disabilities, attitudes towards subjects, and more (see Johnson and Johnson 1998; Johnson, Johnson, and Holubec 2008; Rohrbeck et al. 2003; Slavin 1995, 2010, 2013). This article focuses on research on achievement outcomes of cooperative learning in elementary schools, and on the evidence supporting various theories to account for effects of cooperative learning on achievement.

Theoretical perspectives on cooperative learning

While there is a fair consensus among researchers about the positive effects of cooperative learning on student achievement (Rohrbeck et al. 2003; Roseth, Johnson, and Johnson 2008; Sharan 2002; Slavin 2010, 2013; Webb 2008), there remains a controversy about

---

[†]This article is based on an address at a meeting of the International Association for the Study of Cooperation in Education, Scarborough, England, July 6, 2013.

why and how cooperative learning methods affect achievement and, most importantly, under what conditions cooperative learning has these effects. Different groups of researchers investigating cooperative learning effects on achievement begin with different assumptions and conclude by explaining the achievement effects of cooperative learning in terms that are substantially unrelated or contradictory. In earlier work, Slavin (1995, 2010, 2013) identified motivationalist, social cohesion, cognitive developmental, and cognitive-elaboration as the four major theoretical perspectives on the achievement effects of cooperative learning.

The motivationalist perspective presumes that task motivation is the single most impactful part of the learning process, asserting that the other processes such as planning and helping are driven by individuals' motivated self-interest. Motivationalist-oriented scholars focus more on the reward or goal structure under which students operate. By contrast, the social cohesion perspective (also called social interdependence theory) suggests that the effects of cooperative learning are largely dependent on the cohesiveness of the group. This perspective holds that students help each other learn because they care about the group and its members and come to derive self-identity benefits from group membership (Johnson and Johnson 1989, 1999, 2008). Within this perspective, there is a special case, task specialisation methods, in which students take responsibility for unique portions of a team assignment (Aronson et al. 1978; Sharan and Sharan 1992). The two cognitive perspectives focus on the interactions among groups of students, holding that in themselves, these interactions lead to better learning and thus better achievement. Within the general cognitive heading, developmentalists attribute these effects to processes outlined by scholars such as Piaget and Vygotsky. Work from the cognitive elaboration perspective asserts that learners must engage in some manner of cognitive restructuring (elaboration) of new materials in order to learn them. Cooperative learning is said to facilitate that process.

This article offers a theoretical model of cooperative learning processes as applied in elementary schools which intends to acknowledge the contributions of work from each of the major theoretical perspectives. It places them in a model that depicts the likely role each plays in cooperative learning outcomes. This work further explores conditions under which each may operate, and suggests research and development needed to advance cooperative learning scholarship so that educational practice may truly benefit from the lessons of 30 years of research.

The alternative perspectives on cooperative learning may be seen as complementary, not contradictory. For example, motivational theorists would not argue that the cognitive theories are unnecessary. Instead, they assert that motivation drives cognitive process, which in turn produces learning. They would argue that it is unlikely that over the long haul students would engage in the kind of elaborated explanations found by Webb (2008) to be essential to profiting from cooperative activity, without a goal structure designed to enhance motivation. Similarly, social cohesion theorists might hold that the utility of extrinsic incentives must lie in their contribution to group cohesiveness, caring, and pro-social norms among group members, which could in turn affect cognitive processes.

A simple path model of cooperative learning processes, adapted from Slavin (1995), is diagrammed in Figure 1. It depicts the functional relationships among the major theoretical approaches to cooperative learning.

The diagram of the interdependent relationships among each of the components in Figure 1 begins with a focus on group goals or incentives based on the individual learning of all group members. That is, the model assumes that motivation to learn and to encourage and help others to learn activates cooperative behaviours that will result in learning. This would include both task motivation and motivation to interact in the

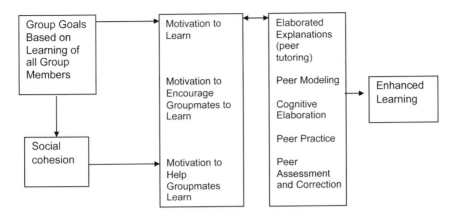

Figure 1. A model of cooperative learning effects on learning.

group. In this model, motivation to succeed leads to learning directly, and also drives the behaviours and attitudes that lead to group cohesion, which in turn facilitates the types of group interactions; peer modelling, equilibration, and cognitive elaboration, that yield enhanced learning and academic achievement. The relationships are conceived to be reciprocal, such that as task motivation leads to the development of group cohesion, that development may reinforce and enhance task motivation. By the same token, the cognitive processes may become intrinsically rewarding and lead to increased task motivation and group cohesion.

Each aspect of the diagrammed model is well represented in the theoretical and empirical cooperative learning literature. All have well-established rationales and some supporting evidence. What follows is a review of the basic theoretical orientation of each perspective, a description of the cooperative learning mode each prescribes, and a discussion of the empirical evidence supporting each.

Four major theoretical perspectives on cooperative learning and achievement

Motivational perspectives

Motivational perspectives on cooperative learning presume that task motivation is the most important part of the process, believing that the other processes are driven by motivation. Therefore, these scholars focus primarily on the reward or goal structures under which students operate (see Slavin 1995). From a motivationalist perspective, cooperative incentive structures create a situation in which the only way group members can attain their own personal goals is if the group is successful. Therefore, to meet their personal goals, group members must both help their groupmates to do whatever enables the group to succeed, and, perhaps even more importantly, to encourage their groupmates to exert maximum efforts. In other words, rewarding groups based on group performance (or the sum of individual performances) creates an interpersonal reward structure in which group members will give or withhold social reinforcers (e.g. praise, encouragement) in response to groupmates' task-related efforts (see Slavin 1983).

The motivationalist critique of traditional classroom organisation holds that the competitive grading and informal reward system of the classroom creates peer norms opposing academic efforts (see Coleman 1961). Since one student's success decreases the chances that others will succeed, students are likely to express norms that high achievement is for 'nerds' or 'teachers' pets'. However, by having students work together towards a common goal, they may be motivated to express norms favouring academic achievement, to reinforce one another for academic efforts.

Not surprisingly, motivational theorists build group rewards into their cooperative learning methods. In methods developed at Johns Hopkins University (Slavin 1994, 1995), students can earn certificates or other recognition if their average team scores on quizzes or other individual assignments exceed a pre-established criterion. Methods developed by David and Roger Johnson (1998; Johnson, Johnson, and Holubec 2008) and their colleagues at the University of Minnesota often give students grades based on group performance, which is defined in several ways. The theoretical rationale for these group rewards is that if students value the success of the group, they will encourage and help one another to achieve.

Empirical support for the motivational perspective

Considerable evidence from practical applications of cooperative learning in elementary schools supports the motivationalist position that group rewards are essential to the effectiveness of cooperative learning, with one critical qualification. Use of group goals or group rewards enhances the achievement outcomes of cooperative learning if and only if the group rewards are based on the individual learning of all group members (Slavin 1995, 2010, 2013). Most often, this means that team scores are computed based on average scores on quizzes which all teammates take individually, without teammate help. For example, in Student Teams-Achievement Divisions, or STAD (Slavin 1994), students work in mixed-ability teams to master material initially presented by the teacher. Following this, students take individual quizzes on the material, and the teams may earn certificates based on the degree to which team members have improved over their own past records. The only way the team can succeed is to ensure that all team members have learned, so the team members' activities focus on explaining concepts to one another, helping one another practice, and encouraging one another to achieve. In contrast, if group rewards are given based on a single group product (e.g. the team completes one worksheet or solves one problem), there is little incentive for group members to explain concepts to one another, and one or two group members may do all the work (see Slavin 1995).

In assessing the empirical evidence supporting cooperative learning strategies, the greatest weight must be given to studies of longer duration. Well executed, these are bound to be more realistically generalisable to the day-to-day functioning of classroom practices. A review of 42 studies of cooperative learning in elementary schools that involved durations of at least four weeks compared achievement gains in cooperative learning and control groups. Of 32 elementary studies of cooperative learning methods that provided group rewards based on the sum of group members' individual learning, 28 (88%) found positive effects on achievement, and none found negative effects (Slavin 1995). The median effect size for the studies from which effect sizes could be computed was +.26 (26% of a standard deviation separated cooperative learning and control treatments). In contrast, eight studies of methods that used group goals based on a single group product or provided no group rewards found few positive effects, with a median effect size of only +.07. Comparisons of alternative treatments within the same studies found similar patterns; group goals based on the sum of individual learning performances were necessary to the instructional effectiveness of the cooperative learning models (e.g. Chapman 2001; Fantuzzo, Polite, and Grayson 1990; Fantuzzo et al. 1989).

Social cohesion perspective

A theoretical perspective somewhat related to the motivational viewpoint holds that the effects of cooperative learning on achievement are strongly mediated by the cohesiveness of the group. The quality of the group's interactions is thought to be largely determined by group cohesion. In essence, students will engage in the task and help one another learn because they identify with the group and want one another to succeed. This perspective is similar to the motivational perspective in that it emphasises primarily motivational rather than cognitive explanations for the instructional effectiveness of cooperative learning. However, motivational theorists hold that students help their groupmates learn primarily because it is in their own interests to do so. Social cohesion theorists, in contrast, emphasise the idea that students help their groupmates learn because they care about the group. A hallmark of the social cohesion perspective is an emphasis on teambuilding activities in preparation for cooperative learning, and processing or group self-evaluation during and after group activities. Social cohesion theorists have historically tended to downplay or reject the group incentives and individual accountability held by motivationalist researchers to be essential. They emphasise, instead, that the effects of cooperative learning on students and on student achievement depend substantially on the quality of the group's interaction (Battisch, Solomon and Delucchi 1993). For example, Cohen (1986, 69–70) stated

> if the task is challenging and interesting, and if students are sufficiently prepared for skills in group process, students will experience the process of groupwork itself as highly rewarding... never grade or evaluate students on their individual contributions to the group product.

Cohen's (1994) work, as well as that of Shlomo Sharan and Yael Sharan (1992) and Elliot Aronson et al. (1978), may be described as social cohesiveness theories. Cohen, Aronson, and the Sharans all use forms of cooperative learning in which students take on individual roles within the group, which Slavin (1983) calls 'task specialisation' methods. In Aronson's Jigsaw method, students study material on one of four or five topics distributed among the group members. They meet in 'expert groups' to share information on their topics with members of other teams who had the same topic, and then take turns presenting their topics to the team. In Sharans' Group Investigation method, groups take on topics within a unit studied by the class as a whole, and then further subdivide the topic into tasks within the group. The students investigate the topic together and ultimately present their findings to the class as a whole. Cohen's (1994) Finding Out/Descubrimiento programme has students play different roles in discovery-oriented science activities.

One main purpose of the task specialisation used in Jigsaw, Group Investigation, and Finding Out/Descubrimiento is to create interdependence among group members. In Johnsons' methods, a somewhat similar form of interdependence is created by having students take on roles as 'checker', 'recorder', 'observer', and so on. The idea is that if students value their groupmates (as a result of teambuilding and other cohesiveness-building activities) and are dependent on one another, they are likely to encourage and help one another to succeed.

Empirical support for the social cohesion perspective

There is some evidence that the achievement effects of cooperative learning depend on social cohesion and the quality of group interactions (Battisch, Solomon, and Delucchi 1993; Johnson and Johnson 2008; Webb 2008). The achievement outcomes of cooperative learning methods that emphasise task specialisation are less clear. Research on the original form of Jigsaw has not generally found positive effects of this method on student achievement (Slavin 1995). One problem with this method is that students have limited exposure to material other than that which they studied themselves, so learning gains on their own topics may be offset by losses on their groupmates' topics. In contrast, there is evidence that when it is well implemented, Group Investigation can significantly increase student achievement (Sharan and Shachar 1988). In studies of at least four weeks' duration, Johnson and Johnson's (2008) methods have not been generally found to increase achievement more than individualistic methods unless they incorporate group rewards (in this case, group grades) based on the average of group members' individual quiz scores (see Slavin 1995). Studies of forms of Jigsaw that have added group rewards to the original model have found positive achievement outcomes (Mattingly and Van Sickle 1991).

Research on practical classroom applications of methods based on social cohesion theories provides inconsistent support for the proposition that building cohesiveness among students through teambuilding alone (i.e. without group incentives) will enhance student achievement. In general, methods which emphasise teambuilding and group process but do not provide specific group rewards based on the learning of all group members are no more effective than traditional instruction in increasing achievement (Slavin 1995), although there is evidence that these methods can be effective if group rewards are added to them (Johnson and Johnson 2008).

Cognitive perspectives

The major alternative to the motivationalist and social cohesiveness perspectives on cooperative learning, both of which focus primarily on group norms and interpersonal influence, is the cognitive perspective. The cognitive perspective holds that interactions among students will in themselves increase student achievement for reasons which have to do with mental processing of information rather than with motivations. Cooperative methods developed by cognitive theorists involve neither the group goals that are the cornerstone of the motivationalist methods nor the emphasis on building group cohesiveness characteristic of the social cohesion methods. However, there are several quite different cognitive perspectives, as well as some which are similar in theoretical perspective, but have developed on largely parallel tracks. The most notable of these are described in the following sections.

Developmental perspectives

One widely researched set of cognitive theories is the developmental perspective (e.g. Damon 1984). The fundamental assumption of the developmental perspective on cooperative learning is that interaction among children around appropriate tasks increases their mastery of critical concepts. Vygotsky (1978, 86) defines the zone of proximal development as '... the distance between the actual developmental level as determined by independent problem solving and the level of potential development as determined through problem solving under adult guidance or in *collaboration with more capable peers*' (emphasis added). In his view, collaborative activity among children promotes growth because children of similar ages are likely to be operating within one another's proximal zones of development, modelling in the collaborative group behaviours more advanced than those they could perform as individuals.

Similarly, Piaget (1926) held that social-arbitrary knowledge –language, values, rules, morality, and symbol systems– can only be learned in interactions with others. Peer interaction is also important in logical–mathematical thought in disequilibrating the child's egocentric conceptualizations and in providing feedback to the child about the validity of logical constructions.

There is a great deal of empirical support for the idea that peer interaction can help non-conservers become conservers. Many studies have shown that when conservers and non-conservers of about the same age work collaboratively on tasks requiring conservation, the non-conservers generally develop and maintain conservation concepts (see Bell, Grossen, and Perret-Clermont 1985). From the developmental perspective, the effects of cooperative learning on student achievement would be largely or entirely due to the use of cooperative tasks. In this view, opportunities for students to discuss, to argue, and to present and hear one another's viewpoints are the critical element of cooperative learning with respect to student achievement.

Empirical evidence for the developmental perspective

Despite considerable support from theoretical and laboratory research, there is little evidence, from classroom experiments conducted over meaningful time periods, that 'pure' cooperative methods, which depend solely on interaction, do produce higher achievement. However, it is likely that the cognitive processes described by developmental theorists are important mediating variables which can help explain the positive outcomes of effective cooperative learning methods (Slavin 1995).

Cognitive elaboration perspectives

A cognitive perspective on cooperative learning quite different from the developmental viewpoint is one which might be called the cognitive elaboration perspective. Research in cognitive psychology has long held that if information is to be retained in memory and related to information already in memory, the learner must engage in some sort of cognitive restructuring, or elaboration, of the material (Callender and McDaniel 2009; Schunk 2012). One of the most effective means of elaboration is explaining the material to someone else. Research on peer tutoring has long found achievement benefits for the tutor as well as the tutee (Calhoon et al. 2007; Mathes, Torgeson, and Allor 2001; Rohrbeck et al. 2003; Thurston et al. 2012; Van Keer 2004). In this method, students take roles as recaller and listener. They read a section of text, and then the recaller summarises the information while the listener corrects any errors, fills in any omitted material, and helps think of ways both students can remember the main ideas. The students switch roles on the next section.

Empirical evidence for the cognitive elaboration perspective

Many brief studies have found that students working on structured 'cooperative scripts' can learn technical material or procedures far better than can students working alone (O'Donnell 2006). While both the recaller and the listener learned more than did students working alone, the recaller learned more. This mirrors both the peer tutoring findings and the findings of Noreen Webb (2008), who discovered that the students who gained the most from cooperative activities were those who provided elaborated explanations to others. Studies of Reciprocal Teaching, in which students learn to formulate questions for each other, have generally supported its positive effects on student achievement (O'Donnell 2000; Palincsar, Brown, and Martin 1987; Rosenshine and Meister 1994; Sporer, Brunstein, and Kieschke 2009).

Structuring group interactions

There is some evidence that carefully structuring the interactions among students in cooperative groups can be effective, even in the absence of group rewards. For example, Meloth and Deering (1992) compared students working in two cooperative conditions. In one, students were taught specific reading comprehension strategies and given 'think sheets' to remind them to use these strategies (e.g. prediction, summarisation, and character mapping). In the other group, students earned team scores if their members improved each week on quizzes. A comparison of the two groups on a reading comprehension test found greater gains for the strategy group.

However, there is also evidence to suggest that a combination of group rewards and strategy training produces much better outcomes than either alone. Fantuzzo, King, and Heller (1992), directly made a comparison between rewards alone, strategy alone, and a combination, and found the combination to be by far the most effective. Further, the outcomes of dyadic learning methods, which use group rewards as well as strategy instruction, produced some of the largest positive effects of any cooperative methods, much larger than those found in studies that provided groups with structure but not rewards. As noted earlier, studies of scripted dyads also found that adding incentives adds to the effects of these strategies (O'Donnell 1996). The consistent positive findings for Cooperative Integrated Reading and Composition (Stevens et al. 1987; Stevens and Slavin 1995a, b), which uses both group rewards and strategy instruction, also argue for this combination.

Reconciling the four perspectives

The model shown in Figure 1 illustrates how group goals might operate to enhance the learning outcomes of cooperative learning. Provision of group goals based on the individual learning of all group members might affect cognitive processes directly, by motivating students to engage in peer modelling, cognitive elaboration, and/or practice with one another. Group goals may also lead to group cohesiveness, increasing caring, and concern among group members and making them feel responsible for one another's achievement, thereby motivating students to engage in cognitive processes which enhance learning. Finally, group goals may motivate students to take responsibility for one another independently of the teacher, thereby solving important classroom organisation problems and providing increased opportunities for cognitively appropriate learning activities. Scholars whose theoretical orientations de-emphasise the utility of extrinsic rewards attempt to intervene directly on mechanisms identified as mediating variables in the model described earlier. For example, social cohesion theorists intervene directly on group cohesiveness by engaging in elaborate teambuilding and group processing training. Cognitive theorists would hold that the cognitive processes that are essential to any theory relating cooperative learning to achievement can be created directly, without the motivational or affective changes discussed by the motivationalist and social cohesion theorists.

From the perspective of the model diagrammed in Figure 1, starting with group goals and individual accountability permits students in cooperative learning groups to benefit from the full range of factors that are known to affect cooperative learning outcomes. While group goals and individual accountability may not always be absolutely necessary, to ignore them would be to ignore the tool with the most consistent evidence of positive effects on student achievement.

In summary, although cooperative learning has been studied in an extraordinary number of field experiments of high methodological quality, there is still much more to be done. Cooperative learning has the potential to become a primary format used by teachers to achieve both traditional and innovative goals. Research must continue to provide the practical, theoretical, and intellectual underpinnings to enable educators to achieve this potential. This article has advanced a cohesive model of the relationships among the important variables involved in the functioning of cooperative learning. It offers a framework for discussion and continued debate while calling for a move towards a unified theoretical model which can guide future research efforts and inform education practice.

References

Aronson, E., N. Blaney, C. Stephan, J. Sikes, and M. Snapp. 1978. *The Jigsaw Classroom*. Beverly Hills, CA: Sage.

Battisch, V., D. Solomon, and K. Delucci. 1993. "Interaction Process and Student Outcomes in Cooperative Learning Groups." *The Elementary School Journal* 94 (1): 19–32.

Bell, N., M. Grossen, and A-N. Perret-Clermont. 1985. "Socio-cognitive Conflict and Intellectual Growth." In *Peer Conflict and Psychological Growth*, edited by M. Berkowitz, 41–54. San Francisco, CA: Jossey-Bass.

Calhoon, M., S. Al Otaiba, D. Cihak, A. King, and A. Avalos. 2007. "The Effects of a Peer-mediated Program on Reading Skill Acquisition for Two-way Bilingual First-grade Classrooms." *Learning Disability Quarterly* 30 (3): 169–184.

Callender, A., and M. McDaniel. 2009. "The Limited Benefits of Rereading Educational Texts." *Contemporary Educational Psychology* 34 (1): 30–41.

Chapman, E. 2001. "More on Moderators in Cooperative Learning Outcomes". Paper presented at the annual meeting of the American Educational Research Association, Montreal, April 19.

Cohen, E. 1986. *Designing groupwork: Strategies for the heterogeneous classroom*. New York: Teachers College Press.

Cohen, E. G. 1994. *Designing Groupwork: Strategies for the Heterogeneous Classroom*. 2nd ed. New York: Teachers College Press.

Coleman, J. 1961. *The Adolescent Society*. New York: Free Press.

Damon, W. 1984. "Peer Education: The Untapped Potential." *Journal of Applied Developmental Psychology* 5 (4): 331–343.

Fantuzzo, J. W., J. A. King, and L. R. Heller. (1992). "Effects of Reciprocal Peer Tutoring on Mathematics and School Adjustment: A Component Analysis." *Journal of Educational Psychology* 84 (3), 133–139.

Fantuzzo, J. W., K. Polite, and N. Grayson. 1990. "An Evaluation of Reciprocal Peer Tutoring Across Elementary School Settings." *Journal of School Psychology* 28 (4): 309–323.

Fantuzzo, J. W., R. E. Riggio, S. Connelly, and L. A. Dimeff. 1989. "Effects of Reciprocal Peer Tutoring on Academic Achievement and Psychological Adjustment: A Component Analysis." *Journal of Educational Psychology* 81 (2): 173–177.

Johnson, D. W., and R. T. Johnson. 1989. *Cooperation and Competition: Theory and research*. Edina, MN: Interaction Book.

Johnson, D. W., and R. T. Johnson. 1998. *Learning Together and Alone: Cooperative, Competitive, and Individualistic Learning*. 5th ed. Boston, MA: Allyn & Bacon.

Johnson, D. W., and R. T. Johnson. 1999. *Learning Together and Alone: Cooperative, Competitive, and Individualistic Learning*. Boston, MA: Allyn & Bacon.

Johnson, D. W., and R. T. Johnson. 2008. "Social Independence Theory and Cooperative Learning: The Teacher's Role." In *The Teacher's Role in Implementing Cooperative Learning in the Classroom*, edited by R. B. Gillies, A. F. Ashman, and J. Terwel, 9–37. New York: Springer.

Johnson, D. W., R. T. Johnson, and E. Holubec. 2008. *Cooperation in the Classroom*. 8th ed. Edina, MN: Interaction Book.

Mathes, P. G., J. K. Torgeson, and J. H. Allor. 2001. "The Effects of Peer-assisted Literacy Strategies for First-grade Readers With and Without Additional Computer-Assisted Instruction in Phonological Awareness." *American Educational Research Journal* 38 (2): 371–410.

Mattingly, R. M., and R. L. Van Sickle. 1991. "Cooperative Learning and Achievement in Social Studies: Jigsaw II." *Social Education* 55 (6): 392–395.

Meloth, M. S., P. D. Deering. 1992. "The Effects of Two Cooperative Conditions on Peer Group Discussions, Reading Comprehension, and Metacognition." *Contemporary Educational Psychology* 17: 175–193. doi:10.1016/0361-476X(92)90057-6

O'Donnell, A. M. 1996. "The Effects of Explicit Incentives on Scripted and Unscripted Cooperation." *Journal of Educational Psychology* 88 (1): 74–86.

LEARNING TO LEARN TOGETHER

O'Donnell, A. M. 2000. "Interactive Effects of Prior Knowledge and Material Format on Cooperative Teaching." *The Journal of Experimental Education* 68 (2): 101–118.

O'Donnell, A. M. 2006. "The Role of Peers and Group Learning." In *Handbook of Educational Psychology*, edited by A. Alexander, and P. H. Winne, 2nd ed., 781–802. Mahwah, NJ: Erlbaum.

Palincsar, A. S., A. L. Brown, and S. M. Martin. 1987. "Peer Interaction in Reading Comprehension Instruction." *Educational Psychologist* 22 (4): 231–253.

Piaget, J. 1926. *The Language and Thought of the Child*. New York: Harcourt Brace.

Rohrbeck, C. A., M. D. Ginsburg-Block, J. W. Fantuzzo, and T. R. Miller. 2003. "Peer-assisted Learning Interventions with Elementary School Students: A Meta-analytic Review." *Journal of Educational Psychology* 95 (2): 240–257.

Rosenshine, B., and C. Meister. 1994. "Reciprocal Teaching: A Review of Research." *Review of Educational Research* 64: 479–530.

Roseth, C. J., D. W. Johnson, and R. T. Johnson. 2008. "Promoting Early Adolescents' Achievement and Peer Relationships: The Effects of Cooperative, Competitive, and Individualistic Goal Structures." *Psychological Bulletin* 134 (2): 223–246.

Schunk, D. 2012. *Learning Theories: An Educational Perspective*. 6th ed. Boston, MA: Allyn & Bacon.

Sharan, S. 2002. "Differentiating Methods of Cooperative Learning in Research and Practice." *Asia Pacific Journal of Education* 22 (1): 31–55.

Sharan, S., and C. Shachar. 1988. *Language and Learning in the Cooperative Classroom*. New York: Springer-Verlag.

Sharan, S., and Y. Sharan. 1992. *Expanding Cooperative Learning Through Group Investigation*. New York: Teachers College Press.

Slavin, R. E. 1983. "When does Cooperative Learning Increase Student Achievement?" *Psychological Bulletin* 94 (3): 429–445.

Slavin, R. E. 1994. *Using Student Team Learning*. 2nd ed. Baltimore, MD: Johns Hopkins University, Center for Social Organization of Schools.

Slavin, R. E. 1995. *Cooperative Learning: Theory, Research, and Practice*. 2nd ed. Boston, MA: Allyn & Bacon.

Slavin, R. E. 2010. "Cooperative Learning." In *International Encyclopedia of Education*, edited by E. Baker, P. Peterson, and B. McGaw, 3rd ed., 161–178. Oxford: Elsevier.

Slavin, R. 2013. "Cooperative Learning and Achievement: Theory and Research." In *Handbook of Psychology*, edited by W. Reynolds, G. Miller, and I. Weiner, Vol. 7, 2nd ed., 199–212. Hoboken, NJ: Wiley.

Sporer, N., J. Brunstein, and U. Kieschke. 2009. "Improving Students' Reading Comprehension Skills: Effects of Strategy Instruction and Reciprocal Teaching." *Learning and Instruction* 19 (3): 272–286.

Stevens, R. J., N. A. Madden, R. E. Slavin, and A. M. Farnish. 1987. "Cooperative Integrated Reading and Composition: Two Field Experiments." *Reading Research Quarterly* 22 (4): 433–454.

Stevens, R. J., and Slavin, R. E. 1995a. "Effects of a Cooperative Approach in Reading and Writing on Academically Handicapped and Nonhandicapped Students." *The Elementary School Journal* 95 (3): 241–262.

Stevens, R. J., and R. E. Slavin. 1995b. "The Cooperative Elementary School: Effects on Students' Achievement, Attitudes, and Social Relations." *American Educational Research Journal* 32 (2): 321–351.

Thurston, A., P. Tymms, C. Merrell, and N. Conlin. 2012. "Improving Achievement Across a Whole District with Peer Tutoring." *Better: Evidence-based Education* 4 (2): 18–19.

Van Keer, H. 2004. "Fostering Reading Comprehension in Fifth Grade by Explicit Instruction in Reading Strategies and Peer Tutoring." *British Journal of Educational Psychology* 74 (1): 37–70.

Vygotsky, L. S. 1978. *Mind in Society*. Edited by M. Cole, V. John-Steiner, S. Scribner, and E. Souberman. Cambridge, MA: Harvard University Press.

Webb, N. M. 2008. "Learning in Small Groups." In *21st Century Education: A Reference Handbook*, edited by T. L. Good, 203–211. Los Angeles, CA: Sage.

The challenges of implementing group work in primary school classrooms and including pupils with special educational needs

Ed Baines, Peter Blatchford and Rob Webster

Psychology and Human Development, Institute of Education, UK

> Findings from two studies are discussed in relation to the experiences and challenges faced by teachers trying to implement effective group work in schools and classrooms and to reflect on the lessons learnt about how to involve pupils with special educational needs (SEN). The first study reports on UK primary school teachers' experiences of implementing a year-long intervention designed to improve the effectiveness of pupils' collaborative group-working in classrooms (the SPRinG [Social Pedagogic Research into Group-work] project). The second study (the MAST [Making a Statement] project) involved systematic observations of 48 pupils with SEN (and comparison pupils) and case studies undertaken in the context of primary school classrooms.

Introduction

There is now a wealth of research on cooperative and collaborative group work that provides persuasive evidence that these approaches are effective in promoting academic attainment, conceptual understanding, pro-social and pro-learning attitudes and communication and social skills (see Lou et al. 1996; Webb and Palincsar 1996; Slavin, Hurley, and Chamberlain 2003). However, much of this experimental research is based on small-scale, short-term studies that are specifically designed and which rarely involve teachers developing and implementing group-work strategies in the everyday context of their own classrooms. Despite this evidence, classroom-based descriptive research has shown that whole-class teaching and independent work are the dominant learning contexts and that group work is relatively rare (Galton, Simon, and Croll 1980; Galton et al. 1999; Kutnick, Blatchford, and Baines 2002; Baines, Blatchford, and Kutnick 2003). These studies suggest that within the majority of primary classrooms, children sit *in* groups, but rarely work together *as* groups. Further evidence suggests that when peer interaction takes place, it is often of low quality (e.g. children may be told to work together – but interactions involve little more than the sharing of answers).

LEARNING TO LEARN TOGETHER

A number of studies have identified resistances to the use of group work (see Baines, Blatchford, and Chowne 2007; Gillies and Boyle 2010). Main concerns amongst teachers are that group work will interrupt or lead to slow coverage of the curriculum; that it will involve the loss of control, increased noise, disruption and off-task behaviour; and beliefs that children cannot work together and are unable to learn from one another or that it is only the more able that can benefit from group work. Many teachers feel that they do group work already whilst also expressing disappointment about its limited value. Students can also be reluctant to get involved in group work because of concerns about teacher expectations and getting the wrong answer (Galton et al. 1999) or because of the possible negative impact on peer relations.

The SPRinG (Social Pedagogic Research into Group Work) research was set up to address these difficulties and resistances to group work. It was also designed to move beyond the limitations of experimental evidence on group work by enabling teachers to use group work under everyday classroom conditions, across the school curriculum and whole-school day. It was a five-year-long project that had two main aims: first, to develop and implement with teachers a programme of principles and activities that incorporated group work into curriculum and everyday school activities (phases one and two); and, second, to evaluate this programme relative to a control group in terms of academic progress, behavioural interaction and dialogue, and attitudes and motivation towards learning (phase three). The overall study covered pupils aged 5–14 years (see Galton et al. 2009; Kutnick and Blatchford 2013). In this paper, we concentrate on research on children between 7 and 11 years (known as Key Stage 2 (KS2).

The resulting programme consisted of a handbook (Baines, Blatchford, and Kutnick 2009) and six training meetings which enabled teachers to develop the skills to use group work across the curriculum. The handbook combined a set of principles and practices along with group skill training activities for pupils that also helped teachers to understand and apply the principles and practices. It aimed to address teachers' and pupils' concerns about group work.

The key principles and recommended practices covered four main areas (see Baines, Blatchford, and Chowne 2007; Kutnick and Blatchford 2013).

(1) Preparing the classroom and group context for group work. This involves arranging the classroom to maximise the potential for group work by thinking about classroom layout, the composition, and size and stability of groups.
(2) Preparing lessons and group-work activities. This involves ensuring that group-work tasks are challenging and warrant group interactions of a high level and involve the application and synthesis of knowledge.
(3) Preparing adults to support pupils and groups. Teachers need to support the groups' ability to do the task rather than directing them on how to do the task through the use of monitoring, guiding (e.g. by asking open-ended questions and offering suggestions), modelling and reinforcing and through coaching.
(4) Preparing pupils for group work. Children do not automatically develop group-working skills and they need to be supported through a 'relational approach' where children feel safe to participate, to ask questions, to discuss problems and to take responsibility for their own learning.

Findings from the evaluation phase of the research were impressive: they showed that relative to a control sample, KS2 SPRinG pupils made greater progress in general science tests at the end of the year. They also made greater progress in specific science lessons that had made extended use of the SPRinG group work. We also found through systematic observation that during group work, SPRinG pupils were more actively engaged in task interactions, were engaged in more sustained interactions and engaged in more high-level reasoning talk (see Blatchford et al. 2006; Baines, Blatchford, and Chowne 2007).

Although these findings represent solid evidence of the benefit of the intervention on pupils, and indicates some overcoming of the resistances to group work identified earlier, informal reports from teachers suggested that a number of challenges remained. These were made most pressing in the case of pupils with Special Education Needs and the difficulties some teachers and pupils experienced during the implementation of group work. We were also interested in finding out how best to enable whole schools to take on group-working practices and to enable a mutually supportive environment for teachers to implement group-work strategies. This fourth phase of the research therefore aimed to examine the experiences and views of school staff involved in implementing the SPRinG programme within their school and classrooms (see Baines 2013). This research provided insights into the challenges of implementing the programme, not revealed by the earlier quantitative results.

The paper brings together findings from this fourth phase of the SPRinG project with relevant results from a second project, the Making a Statement (MAST) project, which involved systematic observations and case studies of children with a statement[1] of Special Educational Needs (SEN) educated in mainstream classroom settings (see Webster and Blatchford 2013a, 2013b). The MAST study was prompted by findings from a large-scale research project on the use and impact of teaching assistants (TAs) which found that pupils with high-level SEN who received high amounts of support from and interaction with TAs had a qualitatively different educational experience from that of their peers (Blatchford, Russell, and Webster 2012). Despite substantial debate on the topic of inclusion, there is little systematic information on the interactions and supports experienced on an everyday basis by pupils with statements in mainstream settings. The main aim of the study was to examine the nature of everyday educational experiences for primary-aged pupils with a statement of SEN. The MAST study provided information on the frequency of interactions pupils with SEN experienced with peers and adults, and the locations and learning contexts within which these occurred. The data from this study provide insights into the opportunities pupils with SEN have for working together with peers in their classrooms.

Specific data from the SPRinG and MAST studies are complementary. The SPRinG study provided insights into the experiences of teachers implementing the programme, and in particular focusing on the challenges and difficulties that they had in the process. One specific tension throughout the research, as we shall see, was how best to involve pupils with SEN. The MAST study enabled a more naturalistic perspective on the extent to which children with SEN are included in mainstream classrooms and are able to participate in, and benefit from, 'peer co-learning' approaches (this term refers to all types of peer learning including cooperative and collaborative learning and peer helping and tutoring – where peers work together to undertake a task). It also offered insights into the factors affecting whether opportunities to work with peers were more or less likely. This paper outlines selected findings from the two studies, as they bear on the challenges involved in implementing peer co-learning. First, it seeks to examine the extent to which children with SEN have opportunities to sit with and interact with peers in everyday classroom contexts, and teachers' views in relation to the SPRinG programme. It then considers possible strategies into what can be done to involve children with SEN in peer co-learning. The paper then moves on to consider the general challenges facing schools, teachers and pupils when implementing a programme of collaborative learning in classrooms. The paper ends by identifying how the implementation of group work can be improved, and how, in particular, pupils with SEN can be meaningfully included within group work.

Method

The SPRinG project

The SPRinG study involved the development with teachers of the collaborative group-work programme and then a systematic evaluation of this programme in relation to a control group. Full details of the study and methods used can be found in Baines, Blatchford, and Kutnick (2008), Blatchford et al. (2006) and Kutnick and Blatchford (2013).

Data collection methods

In the fourth year of the SPRinG research, after the evaluation phase of the study, we asked schools to implement the programme themselves. This was deliberately without the guidance of the research team, but within each school, there was a teacher who had been involved with the programme during the evaluation phase and had implemented group-work in their classrooms for one year. These 'facilitators' agreed to take the lead in working with and supporting colleagues to implement the ideas across the school and in classrooms. All schools received an initial input from a researcher and teacher facilitator at the start of the year which consisted of either an In Service Training afternoon or an extended staff meeting devoted to undertaking and planning for SPRinG implementation.

Teachers' views and experiences were collected via semi-structured interviews at the end of the school year. The interviews were carried out with a sub-sample of 21 facilitators and teachers from seven schools. One group interview with three teachers and a senior member of staff took place due to time constraints and staff availability and there were two written accounts where teachers had not been available. In most cases, interviewees were female (18 out of 21 participants).

The majority of schools were multi-ethnic schools in London with high proportions of children in receipt of Free School Meals (FSM) (mean = 38%, SD = 19), children whose first language was not English (mean = 57%, SD = 34), and children identified as having a Special Educational Need but without a statement (mean = 28%, SD = 10) were higher than the national average.

Interview questions focused on views about the implementation of the programme across the school/Key Stage; their experiences of implementing the ideas into the fabric of the classroom; reflections on the SPRinG ideas and practices and thoughts on what had worked well and what had not worked so well.

The MAST Project

The research involved 48 pupils (9–10 years) drawn from 45 schools in two Local Authorities in the south of England, and four London boroughs. All pupils had a statement of SEN for either moderate learning difficulties (29) or behavioural, emotional and social difficulties (14) with five having a more complex composition of difficulties relating to both areas. Three quarters of the pupils were boys and a quarter were girls and 46% received FSMs. The study also collected data on 151 average attaining pupils of the same gender drawn from the same classrooms to provide a group for comparison.

LEARNING TO LEARN TOGETHER

One of a small team of 15 researchers, trained in the MAST study research methodology, shadowed a pupil with a statement of SEN for a school week, collecting data using a multi-method approach that combined systematic observations of the pupil, with contextual data drawn from interviews with teachers, TAs and parents, and general qualitative observations drawn together into a detailed pupil-based case study.

The systematic observation schedule used was similar to that used in previous studies, including the SPRinG project, and involved a minute-by-minute description of behaviour, interaction and context over the five days. Pupils with SEN were observed for the first 10 seconds in every minute and comparison pupils were observed every fifth minute. This produced a data set of 38,865 data points totalling 648 hours of observation (564 hours for SEN pupils and 83 hours for comparison pupils). This large data set was analysed statistically. Researchers undertook two days of training along with field work practice and reliability (in terms of inter-observer agreement) was high. Full details of training, the methods used and the amount of data collected can be found in Webster and Blatchford (2013a).

Each case study report for the 48 pupils with statements of SEN provided a substantive picture of their educational experiences and covered the organisational factors at the school and classroom level that determined decision-making about provision, the nature and roles of teachers and TAs in this provision, and to what degree this differed from the provision in place for the majority of (non-SEN) pupils. The focus here is on the data from the systematic observations and selected examples from the interview data and from field notes.

Results

Findings from the MAST study are presented first as they reflect the state of play in schools relative to the experiences of pupils with SEN to work together with peers. Results from the SPRinG project will then be presented since these elaborate on the issue relative to the implementation of the group-work programme and suggest some possible solutions.

MAST systematic observation data

The MAST observational data provide important contextual information on the classroom experiences of pupils with SEN. They show that whilst average attaining pupils spent all of their time in class, pupils with a SEN spent over a quarter of their time (27%) outside of the classroom (and therefore 73% of their time in class).

Pupils in classrooms can exist in three main interactional contexts. They can work alone and thus not interact with peers or adults, they can work with an adult, possibly a teacher or a TA on a one-to-one basis or as part of a class or group, or they can work with and interact with peers. Findings showed that pupils with SEN were as likely as comparison pupils to work alone, but they were far more likely than comparison pupils to work and interact with an adult (see Table 1). They were less likely to interact with a teacher than comparison pupils (31% vs. 40%), and far more likely to interact with a TA (27% vs. 2%). In other data not shown in Table 1, it was found that interaction with a TA was during one-to-one interaction (19%) or as part of a group (6%) or class (2%). In contrast, interaction with a teacher was largely within a whole-class instructional context (23%) than a group or one-to-one (4% for each).

Of importance to this paper was the finding that pupils with SEN were half as likely to work with or alongside peers as pupils in the comparison group (18% vs. 32%).

Data on the nature of the grouping context provided further information on the contexts within which pupils with SEN work. As can be seen in Table 2, pupils without SEN were

LEARNING TO LEARN TOGETHER

Table 1. Systematic observation data for pupils with SEN and comparison pupils across the three classroom interactional contexts.

	Comparison		SEN	
Adult and target	42%	1770	58%	17,998
Teacher and target[a]	40%	1677	31%	9555
TA and target[a]	2%	93	27%	8443
Peer and target	32%	1361	18%	5510
No Interaction	26%	1102	24%	7274
Total	100%	4233	100%	30,782

[a]These data are a subset of the Adult and Target data.

Table 2. Systematic observation data relating to the attainment level of the group for pupils with SEN and comparison pupils when observed sitting in groups.

Group attainment	Comparison		SEN	
High	0.4%	11	1%	130
Medium	5%	135	2%	271
Low	5%	151	34%	5782
Mixed	89%	2524	63%	10,603
Total	100%	2821	100%	16,786

most likely to experience mixed attaining groups, yet pupils with SEN were less likely than comparison pupils to experience this setting. More importantly, just over a third of observations of pupils with SEN were of them sitting in low attaining groups, though of course, not necessarily engaged in team working when in these groups.

These patterns may not be particularly surprising, given the range of grouping sizes that can take place in a classroom (e.g. anything from pairs up to the whole class). However, when only the data for small groups of two to six pupils are considered, the picture becomes even more extreme. The comparison group of typical pupils were observed to experience mixed attainment small groups 80% of the time, whilst pupils with SEN experienced them for only 42% of the time. Most importantly, pupils with SEN were observed in low attainment small groups for 57% of the time and comparison pupils only 8% of the time. This highlights the absence of opportunities for pupils with SEN to be able to engage with medium and high attaining peers when learning in mainstream settings.

Results from the MAST case studies

The MAST case studies provide further information on the classroom contexts and dynamics that underpin and help explain the systematic observation results.

Social isolation

The interview and field note data provided evidence of a separation of the pupils with SEN from the rest of the class.

> Pupil 124 seemed to be very socially isolated. She chose to sit alone or away from peers in whole class sessions. When paired with talking partners she was very rarely seen interacting. She was seen keeping herself away from peers.

LEARNING TO LEARN TOGETHER

In other cases, peers were reported to be frightened of, or reluctant to work with, the child with SENs.

> Pupil 122 is very socially isolated within school. As a result of his behaviour, peers are wary of him and were seen actively keeping their distance and asking not to have to work with him.

> TA L explained that the other members of the class may be reticent to work with Pupil 19 because he can rely very heavily upon them to successfully complete tasks, 'he is hard to work with; isn't forthcoming with ideas – so they know if they do work with him they're going to have to do a lot of work themselves. It is a tricky thing, and it is part and parcel of [Pupil 19's] needs … '

Possible reasons for this social isolation include poor social and or communication skills on the part of the pupil with SEN which included: withdrawn or shy behaviour, a dominant, aggressive or confrontational manner, or inappropriate or odd behaviour possibly targeted at trying to improve relations with peers (e.g. overly familiar, affectionate behaviour). Also being at a lower level of attainment in comparison to peers meant that it was difficult for them to engage with peers on tasks set for the class.

But it would be dangerous to attribute the difficulties faced by a number of the target pupils with peer relations to intrinsic qualities of the pupils themselves. One key reason for the relative social disconnect was because of the decisions made about where the child is positioned in the classroom, the extent of interactions with adults, time in and out of the classroom and the general approach to working with the class as a whole and children with SEN.

Peer interaction avoided/discouraged

Interaction with peers might be deliberately reduced because of a perception that the pupil with SEN has problems with peers, and will not benefit from it or that this disrupts the rest of the class or that mainstream peers will miss out on learning and will suffer as a result. This might mean isolating the child or allowing him/her to opt out.

> All staff were concerned that Pupil 16 was having a negative impact on other members of the class. The TA and SENCO talked about the workstation keeping him busy and stopping him 'disturbing anybody'.

> For Pupil 121 peer support was not in use or considered appropriate due to P121's past difficulties working with peers and history of violence/arguments with peers. And: P121 was also allowed to withdraw from group-work to work alone in class when he found it difficult to work with others. Sometimes this was suggested to him by TAs.

There were also concerns about preventing the rest of the class learning.

> Teacher A explained that she chose not to partner Pupil 16 with the same children all the time 'because they are very, very good with him, but it also means they are forever explaining back down to [P16] rather than achieving themselves'. TA L echoed this sentiment saying 'He'd be more of a hindrance to other children sometimes'.

TA proximity restricting opportunities with peers

The systematic observation and case study data are very consistent in showing that a main factor connected to the reduced interactions that target pupils had with other pupils in the class is the tendency for pupils with SEN to be supported by adults, particularly TAs. It is, of course, understandable that schools choose to help pupils with statements by giving them more time with TAs, and in many statements, the extra help to be given to pupils is couched in terms of hours of TA support. But there are, as a result, bound to be implications for the general relationships such pupils have with other pupils. For example, the development of friendships and popularity are often based on proximity and opportunities to interact. Continued presence of a TA may also mean that the pupil with SEN becomes increasingly dependent on this support and thus is likely to become further separated from peers.

Social skills interventions

Related to this are findings from the MAST study which showed the common strategy of seeking to improve a child's social skills is by involving them in individual or group interventions outside of the classroom, and the level of responsibility for this accorded to TAs. There are many social skills interventions and many of these involve concentrated or extended work with an individual child or small group of similarly needy children outside of the classroom. Elements of SEAL (a curriculum focusing on the Social and Emotional Aspects of Learning) require individual work or small group-work with other similar pupils that are conducted away from the classroom context (see Humphrey 2012). Other interventions and individual therapeutic work are also grounded in working only with the individual child and involve the provision of adult-led support. This is not to undervalue these interventions, but rather to suggest that class-based work is as important since this is the context where interactions with peers take place and it is about the development of relationships rather than just skills and reflecting on them. There is also a disconnect in the sense that these skills are worked on outside of the context of their use and leave the children to determine themselves how and whether to apply them once they get back into a classroom context. It appears that there is little strategic thinking about supporting these children's social skills within class.

Findings from SPRinG

Data from the SPRinG project provided more specific information on the use of group-work and pupils with SEN. One might expect that implementing a programme like SPRinG would improve possibilities for children with SEN to engage with peers and there were some indications that this did occur (see Baines 2013). However, a number of teachers talked about the problems they experienced with involving students with social, emotional and behavioural difficulties in group-work. These difficulties involved rejection of the individual by the group as well as disruption caused within the group by the individual. One teacher reported about the difficulties she had had trying to include a child with SEN and discussed the different strategies that she had tried.

> T3: I had a great deal of difficulty last year with B [during SPRinG evaluation phase]. Because absolutely no group wanted to have him because he spoilt every single activity you did, so he was never actually particularly in a group, where he could bond with them, to make much trust. I found it really difficult, and it didn't even help just having him watch a good group and try to pick up ideas that way, he could not apply it and this year I really tried hard not to swap people out of groups because the ones who managed to stay together without any interruptions tended to work better as the year's gone on. (4 teachers, School 4, P9)

Another teacher highlighted the effects that a troubled child with SEN had had on the rest of his group.

> F: ... there was one group with one particularly difficult character, and I kept that character in the same group. Although most of the children had a very positive response to group-work, there were two children specifically in that group that didn't. I thought about moving him halfway through, and perhaps sharing the load in a sense. I think I should have done. I think sometimes it's about having flexibility. (Facilitator, School 5, P1–2)

What can be done?

Deliberate strategies involving peer interaction

The MAST data showed evidence, however, that in some classrooms, pupils with SEN were encouraged to interact and work with mainstream peers without SEN. These could involve the strategic placement of peers to sit near the pupil with SEN and to explicitly work with or support the child with SEN. Sometimes this extended to keeping certain peers away from the child with SEN to avoid arguments and disruption.

Observations and interviews with staff showed that pupils with SEN sometimes worked with peers, either as part of short discussions to input into a whole-class teaching exercise (e.g. talk partners) or as a piece of extended group-work.

> Peer support was used in class with Pupil 18 in a mixed-attaining three rather than a pair for 'talking partners' so that she would be included but could also listen to peers.

Although positive, there were also concerns that pupils with SEN may become overly reliant on these peers and thus close attention was given to ensuring that the child with SEN can actively participate in these interactions.

> The teacher explained to me that [Pupil 7] does have a good relationship with a peer but that there had been concern that he was becoming too reliant, allowing other students to do his work for him. As such she had started swapping talk partners weekly.

There was also evidence that peers received training in the support of a child with SEN.

> Peer support was used with one year six boy providing a lot of peer support in encouraging P117 and building his confidence. This role had been suggested to him by the teachers but he had 'taken it on board' and become an important part of P117's support in the afternoons during foundation subjects.

> TA L: They sometimes find it hard to involve [P19], because if they're in the top group they're quite happy to put forward their opinions – so we tend to just have a chat with them and say ... 'You need to include [P19]. Ask him questions and bring him in' and they're really good with doing that.

One quote from one case study highlights the importance of a positive approach and ethos of inclusion for really helping to include children with SEN and to support their needs.

> Teacher A: The rest of the class are so supportive – I've never come across a more supportive, inclusive class. They are amazing. They would never laugh at him; they're really aware of everyone's different needs of each other, and they are fantastic ... within class you know

LEARNING TO LEARN TOGETHER

with teamwork, he just gets on with it and he just doesn't really notice that anything is different
....

SENCO: His peers are really supportive of him – they know that he has difficulties with things, but they're very good at supporting him and often they'll say, 'Come on [P401], let's do it together'.

Non-SEN peers can also gain from such experiences, both at a level of social sensitivity and understanding and at a cognitive level. It is well established that when more able children help less able children to learn, the more able also benefit since the explanations and thinking required of them help firm up their knowledge (Webb and Palincsar 1996).

Further challenges identified in the SPRinG study

There were further challenges identified by teachers involved in the SPRinG study, which, when handled well, teachers and classes implemented group-work and adapted to the new way of working, but when not handled well, led to a partial implementation of group-work. There were two main themes: school leadership and time, and, control and holding firm.

School leadership and time

According to teachers and facilitators, group-work was most effectively implemented across the whole school when there was a clear planned approach to implementation. This was particularly the case when senior management allowed time for facilitators and teachers to work together to plan the implementation of SPRinG ideas. This involved regular staff discussions during school staff meetings and when group-work was given particular space within curriculum planning meetings between staff. In some schools, time was made available for the facilitating teacher to talk through and model group training activities during planning meetings and in exceptional circumstances to work with other teachers in their classrooms to help them set up group-work and to provide feedback. As one teacher said:

> T: What worked well?. I think the way it's been planned. It's needed somebody to give the information, to act as a reference and to be able to demonstrate. It's having someone who's confident; who understands the process and it's the whole timetabling of it that has worked very well. And I feel by putting it on a timetable, it's shown our commitment towards it. From the Head's ... profiling of it, 'this is really important, we're going to make it work' and having that from the start prevented any worries, panics of scheduling. (Teacher 1, School 6, P1)

Success of implementation was also enhanced when senior management enabled teachers to allot a weekly space in their timetables for SPRinG training activities. This enabled teachers and pupils to have a regular experience of SPRinG training which in turn supported the use of group-work in the curriculum. Allowing teachers to have this time and space made implementation easier. As one teacher reflected:

> T: The school have got to have a massive commitment to it. That might mean dropping other things or ... , its freeing up of time. I think it needs to be a weekly slot. (Teacher 1, School 5 – P7)

Control and 'holding firm'

A number of teachers reported feeling uncertain about group-work because of the reduced sense of control they felt over what children did and learned. Group-work can bring a

LEARNING TO LEARN TOGETHER

perception of a greater distance between teacher and learner because the teacher is rarely present. This can lead to doubts about whether children are talking about the intended issues and a desire to engage in more direct teaching.

> F: I think they [teachers] have to feel confident in the children; that the children can do it. A lot of teachers will feel that they want to control it. It is difficult to let go. Teachers, especially class teachers are in control, and they are guiding everything and I think that's the most difficult thing, letting go, letting your children do it. (Facilitator 1, School 4, P8–9)

Often teachers' concerns were to do with pupils' responses to undertaking group-work, and these were heightened in the case of pupils with difficulties and SEN. These reflected the reasons often given for not doing group-work, reported earlier (e.g. pupils lacking the skills to do group-work, that group-work leads to disruption). An experience that was widely reported by teachers, especially towards the start of implementing SPRinG ideas and often by new or less confident teachers, was of a 'hump' or period of difficulties that led them to feel unsure about the value of group-work. Teachers felt that this was brought on by early emotional tensions and arguments within groups. These teachers reported that if they held firm and continued to support children to resolve their differences themselves, through reflection, then such squabbles would quickly ease and productive group interactions would quickly follow. One teacher wrote about this part of the experience for a SPRinG newsletter.

> F: Now came the difficult part. We watched and supported groups of children as they argued, shouted and sulked. We were very tempted to split them up, but the researchers said it was important that the children worked through these difficulties with adult support. For a long time all we could 'see' was noise and disruption. But after a while we realized that the noise we could hear was actually productive noise. They weren't arguing or talking [off task], they were actively engaged with the work. (Facilitator, School 7, SPRinG Newsletter)

Some teachers, possibly those lacking in confidence, quickly intervened to resolve the problems, for example, to split up the group or even stopping further use of group activities. These responses are understandable, but in order to overcome these barriers, pupils need to have time to adapt and reflect on such difficulties and to develop strategies for managing their feelings and frustrations. How teachers responded to these difficulties appears to be key in determining whether they continued with the regular and substantive use of group-work or whether they made only occasional use of group-work.

The absence of the skills amongst pupils to stem emotionally charged confrontations was one of the most persistent difficulties reported by teachers and experienced by pupils. This can be unsettling for teachers and pupils, particularly pupils with SEN. Helping children to regulate their feelings and to manage conflicts by helping them to take responsibility for their own behaviour and to reflect on and change their own approaches to interaction can make a big difference. Teachers felt that SPRinG training and repeated experiences of group-work led to children being better equipped and more able to deal with these difficulties independently. As one teacher said:

> I: Have you've noticed a change in them (pupils)?

> F: They're more aware of it [being cooperative] because at the beginning ... , if you asked them to work in groups, they'd go 'no, not in groups' because they knew it was going to mean arguments and not getting on, but now they've got some more skills, they can get on better. And you can hear them saying to each other 'come on, you've got to look', 'we've got to get this right',

'we've got to take turns here'. So they know that those skills will help them help themselves. (Facilitator 2, School 4, P2)

Such experiences can be enhanced through the use of stable group compositions. Theories about group development (e.g. Tuckman 1965) would suggest that periods of conflict are not only to be expected but also can be overcome by continued stability in group membership.

Discussion

Findings show that children with SEN often spend a large amount of time outside of the classroom, and even when in the classroom, they are often socially isolated from peers. Despite being educated in mainstream settings, they are not fully included in the social life of school. When pupils with SEN do have opportunities to work with or alongside peers, this is usually with low attaining children or other children with learning difficulties.

Whilst some of this social isolation is due to difficulties that have led to the designation of SEN, much of it may be due to inadvertent or, in some cases, deliberate separation from the class. These children are often viewed as lacking the social skills to engage, and potentially becoming academically dependent on peers or diverting other children's attention away from their learning. The allocation of a TA to work with pupils with SEN inadvertently reinforces separation and may lead to teachers taking less responsibility for planning and involving pupils with SEN in the social and academic activities within class.

There were few occasions where pupils with SEN were allowed to receive support from their peers and to participate in group-work with peers. The case studies suggest that it is possible, though rarely observed, for pupils with SEN to become positively involved with peers in the class and for the class to act as a positive resource for engaging with and supporting pupils with SEN.

Findings from the SPRinG study suggest that successful implementation of a programme of group-work in schools requires a coordinated whole-school approach with committed senior management and a dedicated person to oversee and facilitate its implementation. These are important for allowing teachers to create the time for planning and to support integration of such approaches in to their classrooms, and to enable teachers to observe, try out and get feedback on their practices.

Nevertheless, even with these features in place, implementing group-work into classrooms can still be hard for teachers and pupils. The style of working and the changing teaching and learning environment can ask a lot of both teachers and pupils. Teachers must get used to having less control over the class more generally and over what children learn. Similarly, children need training and guidance in developing the skills that can help them engage in constructive and positive interactions. Such skills include not only speaking, listening, planning and decision-making skills for participating in group-work but also relational skills to help them become more sensitive to and trusting in their classmates. In addition, and this is something not explicitly focused on during the SPRinG programme, is the need to support children in regulating their own emotions and behaviour so that they can prevent themselves from getting upset or angry and so they are better prepared for avoiding and managing petty disputes. Such skills are not easily developed and support through training, repeated experiences and group processing are important features in helping children to adapt. We found that the tensions caused by these challenges can lead teachers to not undertake pupil group-work or can lead to 'SPRinG Lite', a reduced form of SPRinG that may result in less productive interaction and may prolong uncertainties and difficulties amongst pupils and teachers. On the other hand, those teachers who worked through difficulties and supported students found that they got used to working together and that petty squabbles were reduced and resolved independently.

The KS2 children involved in this part of the SPRinG study were having to adapt to new patterns of working and initially found this challenging. Greater use of peer learning approaches from the start of school will better equip pupils to deal with difficult situations (e.g. through self-regulation of emotion and handling of conflict). It is also important that teachers are equipped with the skills and confidence for making use of peer learning approaches as soon as they start teaching. Initial Teacher Training and school-based programmes should provide training in simple and yet effective approaches to peer co-learning which can then be further developed as newly qualified teachers gain confidence in the classroom.

One might have thought that a programme like SPRinG might enhance opportunities for children with SEN to be included within the social life of the class, but here too, despite a few positive accounts, teachers experienced difficulties. Teachers felt that it was difficult to include some pupils with SEN, that their strategies did not always help, that these pupils might get less experience of peer learning, and that often these children find it difficult to develop stable social and working relationships with peers. This is worrying because many of these pupils with SEN have an important need for the development of social skills and relationships and to be fully included in mainstream settings. There are no easy solutions or strategies for involving pupils with SEN and it would be difficult to arrive at a 'one-size-fits-all' solution, not the least because these pupils vary widely in their characteristics and needs. It is essential that further research examine the experiences of children with SEN both during group-work and within the wider classroom context, to help identify practices and strategies for effectively involving them in peer learning and classroom life.

Currently, there are a range of interventions, both individual and group-based, that aim to support the development of social and emotional skills, coping and mental health. The MAST study showed that these interventions are often undertaken outside of the classroom with little strategic thinking about how the skills can be further supported, applied or enhanced in the classroom and wider school contexts (e.g. the playground). The child is left with the task of transferring and applying this learning into the classroom context. Furthermore, such training is largely talk-based and therapeutic, yet involves little 'doing' and is likely to be reflective rather than involving planning and strategic thinking. One clear way of providing useful opportunities for children with SEN to develop the social and behavioural skills they need is by involving them in regular group interaction and peer learning within the classroom context. Teachers need to think strategically about involving and supporting pupils with SEN through interactions with peers, rather than isolating these children, preventing them from getting involved or passing them around groups. Their classmates are also likely to benefit in the process, not only from having to work with, adapt to and be sensitive to such pupils but also from the inclusive attitudes and ethos that would be enhanced by the greater involvement of pupils with SEN.

We should not underestimate the challenge facing teachers and schools. Teaching children and fostering positive learning experiences are by no means straightforward and there are many pressures on schools to perform and to cover a prescribed curriculum. Incorporating peer learning strategies and group-work into everyday classroom learning can raise difficulties and challenges that can appear to detract from these wider pressures on schools. But if we are to furnish pupils with the skills to work together with others (as they have to in most communities and work places), to be tolerant of others, to celebrate

LEARNING TO LEARN TOGETHER

individual diversity and to enhance an enduring depth to learning and knowledge, then peer learning approaches for *all* pupils need to be a central part of pedagogic practices that teachers utilise for enhancing learning in the twenty-first century.

Funding

This research was supported by the Economic and Social Research Council [grant number [L139251046]] and the Nuffield Foundation.

Note

1. In England, a 'statement' is provided by the Local Education Authority and indicates that to meet a child's special educational needs, additional provision, beyond the everyday resources and provision that a school has, is required.

References

Baines, E. 2013. "Teachers' Experiences of Implementing the SPRinG Programme in Schools." In *Effective Group-Work in Primary School Classrooms: The SPRinG Approach*, edited by P. Kutnick, and P. Blatchford, with E. Baines and A. Tolmie, 149–184. London: Springer.

Baines, E., P. Blatchford, and A. Chowne. 2007. "Improving the Effectiveness of Collaborative Group-Work in Primary Schools: Effects on Science Attainment." ESRC Teaching and Learning Research Programme Special Issue of the *British Educational Research Journal* 33 (5): 663–680.

Baines, E., P. Blatchford, and P. Kutnick. 2003. "Changes in Grouping Practices in Classrooms: Changing Patterns over Primary and Secondary Schooling." *International Journal of Educational Research* 39 (1/2): 9–34.

Baines, E., P. Blatchford, and P. Kutnick. 2008. "Pupil Grouping for Learning: Developing a Social Pedagogy of the Classroom." In *The Teacher's Role in Implementing Cooperative Learning in the Classroom*, edited by R. Gillies, A. Ashman, and J. Terwel, 56–72. New York: Springer-Verlag.

Baines, E., P. Blatchford, and P. Kutnick, with A. Chowne, C. Ota, and L. Berdondini. 2009. *Promoting Effective Group Work in the Classroom: A Handbook for Teachers and Practitioners*. London: Routledge.

Blatchford, P., E. Baines, C. Rubie-Davies, P. Bassett, and A. Chowne. 2006. "The Effect of a New Approach to Group-Work on Pupil-Pupil and Teacher-Pupil Interactions." *Journal of Educational Psychology* 98 (4): 750–765.

Blatchford, P., A. Russell, and R. Webster. 2012. *Reassessing the Impact of Teaching Assistants: How Research Challenges Practice and Policy*. Oxon: Routledge.

Galton, M. J., L. Hargreaves, C. Comber, D. Wall, and A. Pell. 1999. *Inside the Primary Classroom: 20 Years On*. London: Routledge.

Galton, M. J., B. Simon, and P. Croll. 1980. *Inside the Primary Classroom*. London: Routledge and Kegan Paul.

Galton, M., S. Steward, L. Hargreaves, C. Page, and A. Pell. 2009. *Motivating Your Secondary Class*. London: Sage.

Gillies, R. M., and M. Boyle. 2010. "Teachers' Reflections on Cooperative Learning: Issues of Implementation." *Teaching and Teacher Education* 26 (4): 933–940.

Humphrey, N. 2012. "The Social and Emotional Aspects of Learning (SEAL) Programme." In *Bad Education: Debunking Myths in Education*, edited by Philip Adey and Justin Dillon, 143–160. Maidenhead: OUP.

Kutnick, P., P. Blatchford, and E. Baines. 2002. "Pupil Groupings in Primary School Classrooms: Sites for Learning and Social Pedagogy." *British Education Research Journal* 28 (2): 187–206.

Kutnick, P., and P. Blatchford, with E. Baines and A. Tolmie. 2013. *Effective Group-Work in Primary School Classrooms: The SPRinG Approach*. London: Springer.

Lou, Y., P. Abrami, J. Spence, B. Chambers, C. Poulsen, and S. d'Apollonia. 1996. "Within-Class Grouping: A Meta-Analysis." *Review of Educational Research* 66 (4): 423–458.

Slavin, R., E. A. Hurley, and A. Chamberlain. 2003. "Cooperative Learning and Achievement: Theory and Research." In *Handbook of Psychology: Educational Psychology*, edited by W. M. Reynolds and G. E. Miller, 7 vols, 177–198. New York: Wiley.

Tuckman, B. 1965. "Developmental Sequence in Small Groups." *Psychological Bulletin* 63 (6): 384–399.

Webb, N. M., and A. S. Palincsar. 1996. "Group Processes in the Classroom." In *Handbook of Educational Psychology*, edited by D. C. Berliner and R. C. Calfee, 841–873. New York: Macmillan.

Webster, R., and P. Blatchford. 2013a. *The Making a Statement Project Final Report: A Study of the Teaching and Support Experienced by Pupils with a Statement of Special Educational Needs in Mainstream Primary Schools*. Report for Nuffield Foundation.

Webster, R., and P. Blatchford. 2013b. "The Educational Experiences of Pupils with a Statement for Special Educational Needs in Mainstream Primary Schools: Results from a Systematic Observation Study." *European Journal of Special Education* 28 (4): 463–479.

Status problem and expectations of competence: a challenging path for teachers

Isabella Pescarmona

Department of Education, University of Turin, Turin, Italy

> Complex Instruction (CI) is a cooperative learning approach, which aims at improving the equal status interaction among students working in groups who may be at different academic and social levels. Based on an ethnographic research, the article examines how a group of Italian primary school teachers understand the status problem and how the finding from this research demonstrates a change in their expectations of competence through using CI. This research analyses to what extent these teachers meet the original goal of achieving greater equity, as well as discussing implications for teachers' professional development.

Introduction: status problem and participation in cooperative groups

During the last decades, the process of globalisation with its social and cultural changes has brought about a general reflection on the growing diversity in the classroom, and on the role of education in our complex societies. The requirements of Lisbon Strategy (CEC 2000; High Level Group, 2004) highlight the importance of a more inclusive and effective educational process. These entail the provision of equal opportunities for all students in educational activities and in classroom interactions, regardless of their cultural and social backgrounds. Complex Instruction (CI) is one of the ways of creating the conditions for such a process to take place.

This strategy is a cooperative learning approach developed by Elizabeth Cohen and her staff at Stanford University, California, with the specific aim of improving the equal status interaction between students of differing academic and social levels in group work (Cohen 1994; Cohen and Lotan 1997a, 2004). Cohen points out that differences in students' participation also occur within cooperative groups. Even here, some members tend to be more active and influential than others. Cohen explains this situation in terms of status problem, starting from a sociological analysis of interactions in classrooms and Expectation States Theory (Rosenthal and Jacobson 1972; Rosenholtz and Rosenholtz 1981; Simpson 1981).

The status problem is defined as 'an agreed-upon social ranking where everyone feels it is better to have a high rank within the status order than a low rank' (Cohen 1994, 27). Examples of status features are race, social class, sex, reading ability and attractiveness.

LEARNING TO LEARN TOGETHER

These could affect what happens in small groups. Low-status students often do not have access to the task, they sometimes cannot put their hands on materials and they are frequently physically separated from the rest of the group. They do not talk as much as other students. In solving group tasks, high-ranking members usually do most of the talking. So they are seen as more competent, and as having done more to lead the group, whereas those who are relatively quiet are seen as having made little contribution. In accordance with the Expectation States Theory (Rosenthal and Jacobson 1972; Rosenholtz and Rosenholtz 1981; Simpson 1981), different expectations of competences of different students produce different interactions and learning achievements within the group. These can produce a kind of self-fulfilling prophecy where higher-status students always hold the highest ranks in the status order, while low-status students invariably hold the lowest. Pupils benefit from talking and explaining to others, and high-status pupils usually speak more than low-status classmates (Cohen 1994). Putting it briefly, the more you talk, the more you learn, the less you talk, the less you learn. Teachers may mistakenly see low-status students as passive or uninvolved, whereas they are simply unable to get access to the materials or the attention of the group. Teachers may also interpret this problem in terms of unfriendliness and distrust, but a group can be very friendly and trusting and still exhibit a sharp status order, with some members perceived as much more competent that others (Cohen 1994). According to Cohen, the status problem is based on different expectations of competence and teachers should consciously act on these.

In order to make cooperation in small groups successful, Cohen created a strategy to modify students' and teachers' expectations of competence and make group learning situations more equitable. This strategy emphasises the development of higher-order thinking skills, thanks to the creation of a multiple ability task designed around an open question (a *Big Idea*). In order to be solved, it should be approached from different perspectives and involve a rich variety of skills and intelligences (Gardner 1983). This requires teachers to delegate their authority by using cooperative roles and rules and organise students in heterogeneous groups. Not only do teachers have to create a rich cooperative task, but they also have to convince students that the task involves many different intellectual abilities, which requires the contribution of each member. This entails assigning a positive and appropriate feedback to low-status students, based on teachers' observations of group work, to underline the relevant intellectual contributions that each group member gives to the task solution. In this way, CI explicitly aims at developing a mixed set of expectations of intellectual competences for each student, thus changing the concept of what it means to be 'smart'.

Most studies on status treatment focus on the evaluation of its effectiveness in quantitative terms (Cohen 1997; Cohen and Lotan 1997b; Ellis and Lotan 1997). These rarely explore the process of assuming a different perspective in the usual teaching style and beliefs by taking on a qualitative approach (Perrenet and Terwel 1997). Status treatment is a key concept of CI strategy. Therefore, it seems relevant to investigate the teachers' point of view, as their ideas may affect the implementation of the strategy in class. The teachers' perspective had already emerged as a crucial element which should not be taken for granted (see Gobbo 2007; Pescarmona 2010, 2011a, 2012).

This study aims at investigating: how a group of Italian primary school teachers interpreted the status problem; what criteria they use to define high- and low-status students; and how they implemented status treatment in classrooms. Finally, it reflects on how these teachers changed their expectations of competence in order to meet the original goal of equity.

Research context and methodology

This study is part of a wider research project on educational innovation. It explores what it means for teachers and their students to implement CI at school, and if and how the school context may change.

The research project involved six Italian primary school teachers of different subjects in Bologna and its Province. They decided to experiment with CI in their classrooms after a teacher-training course, which took place in 2004–2005 (Augelli, Gobbo, Pescarmona, and Traversi 2005). This was one of the first experiences on CI in Italy. Data were collected using an ethnographic methodology. Open interviews, participant observation and informal conversations were employed in teachers' meetings, while they were creating new CI teaching units, and in the classroom during the CI experiments. The main fieldwork for this study was undertaken from December 2006 to May 2008, at least twice a month. This research mode is defined as 'a recurrent time mode' (Jeffrey and Troman 2006), which emphasises on systemised field visits and ongoing narrative in order to ascertain the similarity and the differences over time of processes and provide a 'thick description' (Geertz 1987) of the school context involved. During the research process, the author took on a dual role: supervisor of teachers' work and researcher. As a supervisor, I took part in teacher meetings and facilitated the construction of new teaching units according to CI principles. However, as a researcher, I took field notes on interactions and discussions which occurred during these meetings, and then during the CI experiment in class. Thus, I adopted an 'observing participation' (Sansoè 2007; Pescarmona 2011b) rather than a participant observation. Sometimes this was not easy: the extensive involvement in the task and the close relationship with these teachers could undermine the principle of 'making the familiar strange' (see Mills 1959). Reading other ethnographic research projects and taking a personal diary on methodological issues were helpful for developing reflexivity (Pescarmona 2012). However, at the same time, this balancing position between distancing and participating provided me with the opportunity to observe and listen to teachers' questions, choices and struggles, which they encountered in adopting the CI strategy (on this point see Pescarmona 2011a, 2012). I kept a fieldwork diary, but many times I relied on dialogues and considerations that I had heard and quickly noted in the field, and transcribed at home. In fact, extensive data were collected in class, but sometimes the most relevant comments came out during conversations with teachers in the staff room and in their houses. It was especially at home, in fact, that teachers planned the cooperative activities and more freely expressed their doubts, feelings and interpretations, especially regarding low-status students. The key strength of ethnography is that it contributes to the understanding of teachers' (and pupils') perspectives and highlights the meanings they give to their experience related to the cultures and organisations studied (Hargreaves and Woods 1984; Walford 2002; Troman, Jeffrey and Walford 2004). The observations and social interactions were qualitatively analysed using a grounded theory approach (Glaser and Strauss 1967). I reflected upon empirical data by coding and recording them in order to create interpretative categories, and tested these in the field.

In this article, I focus on these research questions: how teachers understand and implement status treatment in their multicultural classrooms and to what extent they develop their professional identity.

Teachers' perception of the status problem

Since the beginning of this study, the teachers stated that they were 'fascinated' by the Status and Expectation theory and by Cohen's status treatment approach. They recognised the value of the goal of equity as a part of their professional identity and appreciated the explanations of unequal participation in terms of the status problem. Even though they implemented active learning activities and adopted a creative teaching style, they realised that status problems also occurred in their classes and had to be tackled. They were responsible for the inclusion of their students in classroom activities and thus were very motivated to translate the abstract understanding of Cohen's strategy into practice in their classes. However, findings revealed that they coped with status theory in a complex way.

According to Cohen, they recognised that a different ethnic origin or belonging to a lower social class could provide students with a low status. For example, two of these teachers worked in an area with a high degree of immigration and stated that pupils coming from different countries often were enrolled in school during the year and learnt Italian for the first time. Many times, they spent one or two years there and then moved with the family to big cities. These pupils (and families) did not benefit from a fair treatment in classroom and within the community. However, in the teachers' opinions, Cohen's theory was not sufficient to explain differences in students' participation in class and in small groups. They believed it was important to 'complete' Cohen's perspective with their own educational ideas. In their opinion, what played a crucial role was the complex existential dimension of each child and the relative relational difficulties and peer tensions. They explained these by taking into consideration how each pupil settled into the class. One teacher spoke about 'Pupils who did not fit in well in the class' and another described that, in the case of peer tensions, 'some pupils do not know how to cope with frustration or overcome it'. They often reported that pupils were highly emotional and had difficulty in recognising others' needs and points of view. From this perspective, a teacher even stated 'In my class, the problem are high status pupils,' as they spent most of the time arguing with each other about who was right and completely ignored the other students' opinions. Sometimes teachers tried to explain this by considering the young age of the children and emphasising the importance of the emotional aspect in teaching in primary schools. Other times, they referred to the particular background of some families by pointing out how difficult managing school requirements might be for some parents. All this could make pupils insecure and distracted in class.

The teachers believed that some pupils' characteristics and certain family situations could have a detrimental effect on the relationships between students and, therefore, undermine their academic achievements. For this reason, they perceived their role as mediators of relational and emotional difficulties and, from this perspective, they interpreted the goal of providing equal opportunities in terms of 'integrating difficult pupils' and 'mediating conflicts in class'. They said their role was 'giving all students the same tools to get on at school and in society' and 'promoting pupils' self-esteem' to enable students to participate.

The teachers recognised status criteria and the goal of equity promoted by Cohen's theory, but they felt challenged by the task of combining them with their own professional experience and educational purposes, which also took into account other aspects. As a result, they tended to give a wider meaning to the status problem and carried out different strategies in their own classrooms.

Strategies and dilemmas in coping with the status problem

Strategies in planning CI activities

The teachers' idea of status developed during the planning of CI experiments in class. CI requires teachers to organise groups by assigning different roles (such as *facilitator*, *reporter*, *materials manager*, *timekeeper* and *group harmoniser*) and by mixing pupils according to their various abilities in order to create efficient and effective groups. The Bologna teachers took this stage of the strategy very seriously, spending a long time on forming each group and on reflecting how to assign the different cooperative group roles. They tried to form heterogeneous but 'welcoming' groups, where low-status pupils could feel free to join in. They placed 'difficult' and 'quarrelling' pupils in different groups, by taking into account the various friendships between students. They chose to assign appropriate activities to each student or group, by considering the multiple abilities required by the task. Moreover, before implementing CI teaching units, these teachers devoted a lot of time to teach social skills by means of games and activities widely practised in cooperative learning, which Cohen refers to as *skillbuilders* (Cohen 1994). They managed CI organisation very well and adopted the new ideas in line with their previous educational scope of socialisation (a critical reflection on the development of social skills is presented in Pescarmona, 2014).

By planning CI activities, the teachers had the opportunity to reflect on this previous idea and on their perception of low-status students. During work meetings and informal conversations, they expressed their uncertainties and reflections. They were concerned about the ability of some pupils to work on their own and cope with frustration in case of failure. The main doubt was 'Will they be able to do that?' or 'Will pupils work out a solution in time?' They often gave the simplest activities to groups considered the weakest. For example, among the different CI activities they created, they selected those that do not require reading a lot, but are mainly based on discussing pictures or listening to a song. They also tended to assign low-status students group roles that were thought to be easier, such as *timekeeper* or *material manager*, because, as a teacher explained, 'It is clearer for them to understand what they have to do.' Roles such as *facilitator* or *reporter* were given to high-status pupils, mainly because these required linguistic and logic skills, which were considered to be more difficult.

However, while wanting to make things easier for some pupils, the teachers realised that in this way some learning opportunities were denied to them. They discussed 'Each pupil must have the opportunity of experimenting' and 'There is no way of knowing in advance how they managed the cooperative task.' Driven by Cohen's status theory, the teachers became more aware of their own expectations of the students' competence. They considered the risk related to pigeonholing some students and their supposed abilities beforehand: students could interact with each other in a stereotypical way rather than interdependently, where each of them could give an original contribution, and some groups could perceive themselves as 'no good'. By doing so, the same class hierarchy might be re-established, which is exactly what CI wanted to overcome.

Hence, they decided to rotate roles and activities in class, and reflected on the need to observe and recognise the real abilities of each child. They wanted to trust pupils' capacities: 'Complex Instruction is a real challenge for pupils!' declared one of them. They decided to take the risk of delegating their authority and give students the chance to succeed. The role which teachers found the most critical to assign was the *group harmoniser* because it entails the ability of mediating peer tensions, which teachers still considered as one of the most problematic aspects.

Assigning competence to low-status students

Assigning competence to low-status students was the step that really called into question teachers' previous educational ideas. Giving such a positive public feedback represents a powerful means to modify teachers' and classmates' expectations of competence. As Cohen says, it is not enough to develop a multiple ability curriculum without a clear

LEARNING TO LEARN TOGETHER

intervention on students' expectations. 'Students should not only appreciate the differing perspectives and cultures of their classmates but also feel that they are on an equal footing with each other intellectually and academically' (Cohen and Lotan 2004, 737).

The Bologna teachers understood that assigning competence to low-status students was the key to helping low-status students in small group settings, and so devoted a significant part of the CI experiment to it. They provided very good feedback on social abilities and cooperative roles by discussing the children's behaviour in groups. They pointed out which cooperative rules were more suitable in a group situation, and discussed how pupils could improve the group effectiveness. They highlighted the benefit of using some social abilities, such as 'every member of each group is responsible for all work', 'asking for others' opinions' or 'allowing everyone to contribute', and supported the discussion by implementing an evaluation grid for these new abilities. These teachers knew that learning how to work in a group is a result of a training process, where these norms must be labelled, discussed and practised (see Bandura 1969; Cohen 1994). The attention devoted to this aspect was so important that even one of the pupils, a nine-year-old boy (fourth-year class), decided to create his own evaluation grid. This process of internalisation of new social norms met their educational purposes of improving peer relationships and created a more productive atmosphere in their classes.

What these teachers found much harder was giving low-status students a feedback in terms of multiple intelligences. This term refers to the current work on reconceptualising human intelligence, which is seen as multiple and rooted in specific areas of the brain (see Sternberg and Spear-Swerling 1966; Gardner 1983). In order to be effective, status treatment requires teachers, first, to convince the students that many different intellectual abilities are necessary for solving the group work task and, second, to publicly evaluate a low-status student as being strong in a particular multiple ability. This recognition creates a mixed set of expectations for each student and translates into a positive expectation for future group work. But putting this principle into practice was more difficult to manage than teachers would have expected. The Bologna teachers expressed a feeling of 'inadequacy' and often said 'Feedback is my weak point.' They were aware of the power that is involved in providing a feedback on specific intellectual contributions, such as conceiving an idea for an illustration, designing an object or figuring out how the workings of a certain mechanism. But they often spoke more in general terms about 'creativity'. Sometimes the teachers proposed to edit a list of the multiple abilities required by each task; however they learnt that that again entailed pigeonholing students' abilities beforehand. They also expressed their concern about some pupils' abilities and complained, 'CI might make things hard for low status students. Their problems arise during the activities.' Assigning competence brought up one of their crucial educational points, 'We have to find a balance between not causing frustration to pupils with high level problem tasks, and convincing them that they are able to learn and solve the task.'

Thus, teachers described their own struggle in finding opportunities to assign competences to students and blamed their frustration on the difficulty of having to observe what happened in more than one or two groups simultaneously. Whenever they found themselves in difficulty they would resolve it saying 'What is important is recognizing the positive things that emerge.' By doing so, they resisted new ideas and tended to come back to the usual way of evaluating.

However, these teachers recognised that status treatment was at the core of the strategy and they searched for a solution. By dealing with it, they reflected on their usual way of evaluating students in a more critical way, 'Are we considering some students less able to learn?' and tried to find new strategies to cope with status treatment in a successful way. A teacher chose to allocate extra time to develop the group's final presentation by underlining the multiple abilities involved. Another teacher decided to take notes and

31

present the assignments of competence during the following days. By doing so, they also called into question their teaching style, 'Am I giving enough space to bring to light and recognize the different contributions of each student?' and expressed the need to extend their evaluation criteria into everyday lessons, because 'Students' status comes out from your teaching method.' They felt they had the power to change and work in a different way. They were transforming their educational perspective. Therefore, CI became an opportunity for reflecting on their usual way of teaching.

The process of modifying their expectations was not completely resolved. They 'fluctuated' between the new ideas and those that they were accustomed to (see Pescarmona 2010, 2011a). Sometimes the teachers gave positive feedback in terms of multiple abilities, and it was a success for the participation of low-status students. For example, a teacher gave a specific and relevant feedback to a lower-achieving pupil, who composed a beautiful song, and another teacher recognised the useful contribution of a little girl, who created appropriate clothes for her group's drama by collecting information about life in the past. Other times, they went back to their usual way of evaluating social abilities or replaced the recognition of the intellectual contribution of each student with a more general 'giving voice to everyone'. Their usual strategies were correct in a general sense, but they did not go strictly in the direction recommended by Cohen.

The challenge of evaluation

The process of implementing status treatment was not easy and was not to be taken for granted. Feedback on multiple intelligences explicitly required teachers to modify their expectations. While during CI group task teachers have to delegate authority, feedback depends solely on the teachers' evaluation, calling into question their prejudices. Therefore, it was not unusual for Bologna teachers to feel uncomfortable. Developing multiple perceptions about pupils needs to be an intentional choice. This entails being ready to recognise and underline the different intelligences and abilities that may emerge, so as to give students the opportunity to enhance their status. This contributes to creating a more democratic environment. This is because *evaluating students* is different from *assigning competences to students*. *Evaluating* requires that teachers act according to a previously defined system of criteria; they have the power to ascribe the status to students. On the other hand, *assigning competences to students* requires that teachers recognise and underline the contribution that each student makes. This is not a previously defined criterion, but a process in which students have a chance to succeed and show their own abilities more freely. In this way, students are given the opportunity to become partly responsible for their own status. In this perspective, not only was status treatment a challenge for the pupils, but it was also a challenge for the teachers. Indeed, CI could become an opportunity for changing the usual way of looking at pupils in class, and may provide an alternative way of assessing them based on multiple intellectual abilities.

Teachers and the goal of equity: some reflections

During the whole process, the Bologna teachers were aware that CI was not 'somewhat magical', but it required that they work hard to create opportunities to identify low-students' strengths. It meant undertaking a deep professional change. The question was to what extent this met the original goal of equity.

Some critical points emerged in dealing with the status problem, such as the emphasis on social abilities, the importance given to the mediation of conflict in class, and the effort to recognise students' different intellectual contributions and give appropriate feedbacks. These were not to be considered lightly. They can shed light on how these teachers interpreted the issue of equity and social justice at school. In fact, during the implementation of status treatment they experienced a dilemma. It seems that their idea of equity oscillated between (1) a promotion of social competences for living and working together in peace and (2) the recognition of the equal rights for each pupil to give their contribution. Both of these are worthwhile perspectives, but there are some differences. The former expects teachers to have a crucial role in managing relationships and supporting the personal development of each student. This was the perspective Bologna teachers were more accustomed to. The latter, introduced by Cohen, considers teachers as a part of the status problem because of their expectations – and a part of their solution, too. It aims at changing their own perceptions. The final aim of these two positions is also different. While the first idea assumes that schools should develop pupils as humane and liberal people, who are aware of their relationships with the rest of humanity, the second idea emphasises that schools should help students to become active citizens capable of participating and giving their own contribution to change society. This view can be more revolutionary than the first, since it aims directly at having students' (and future citizens') voices heard, and may change a future status order.

This dilemma may be related to the way in which progressive education and the relative educational innovation took place in Italy. Despite having been developed during the first decades of the twentieth century, mainly in Anglo-Saxon countries, these new educational ideas reached the Italian context much later, after the Second World War (Allemann-Ghioda 2000), and had to deal with a different and complex socio-political context. Some research (Allemann-Ghionda 2000; Gonon 2000; Oelkers 2000) highlights that the reception of progressive education was influenced by the main ideologies of the first half of the twentieth century. The Italian cultural and educational context of that period was affected by fascism, then by communist and socialist philosophy and further on by the Catholic Church and its pedagogy, which was based on personalism taken from J. Maritain (on this point see Chiosso 1997). These did not reject the principles of progressive education (such as the emphasis on learning by doing, the focus on individual students' needs and self-expression, the centrality given to problem-solving, critical thinking and group work), but rather selected some of its elements and integrated them into mainstream education. During this process, it seems that progressive education had been filtered from the original political question of democratic participation. It had preserved the idea of coexistence within civic society, but under the state control (which was represented at school by the teacher's power). In Italy, the educational debate seems to have emphasised idealistic principles, such as 'social responsibility', 'human solidarity' and 'social education', based on the individual psychological development of each child, rather than the scope of forming good future citizens, who will be able to actively contribute to the improvement of society. Hence, one of the principal benefits of Cohen's legacy is that it contributes to bring the issues of equity and democratic participation back to the core of the educational debate today.

Conclusion

When instructional methods are complex and demanding, such as CI, teachers need to develop a more general and theoretical way of understanding their roles (Cohen et al. 2004). During the process of experimenting with status treatment the Bologna teachers had significant positive experiences. However, they questioned whether, when and how to intervene. They had to make non-routine decisions rather than follow a pre-arranged plan. They were required to consider multiple factors, to control the classroom and to have sufficient observation skills. But treating the status problem was not only a matter of competence. The research data clearly show that it was a true 'process of appropriation' (Pescarmona 2011a, 2011b, 2012). This ethnographic research did not give quantitative data and outcomes, but it provided a rich qualitative interpretation and evaluation of the process by considering the perspective of comparative education studies (Philips and Ochs 2004; Steiner-Khamsi 2004), which discuss the complex process of 'borrowing' ideas and practices from elsewhere. These teachers did not develop Cohen's status treatment as a 'ready-to-use' package. They interwove the new ideas with their own educational perspectives. They acted according to their own educational ideas and the cultural context in which they worked. They did not just follow a format, but they gave a new meaning to status issue in relation to this 'culture of the school' (Florio-Ruane 1996) and teaching tradition (on this point see Pescarmona 2011a). An analysis of this process of appropriation is essential, not only as an external justification, but as a means to going beyond an ideological re-framing of status issue. Indeed, the status problem is not something to be taken for granted, but is something to be questioned every time and evaluated in fieldwork. It is not to be considered as a 'ready-to-use' package, a way of labelling students. Its strength lies in the fact that it calls teachers and their expectations into question. Only by reflecting on this category will teachers be able to move closer to the goal of equity.

This study shows that this process of appropriation and reflection had positive implications for the professional development of teachers, in terms of social justice. First, it made these teachers more conscious of the status problem. Second, it promoted the teachers' ability of observing their students by developing multiple expectations. It led them to evaluate students on multiple dimensions, which is the basis for inclusive teaching despite the great diversity of academic skills. This is a professional innovation which is required of teachers in our complex and multicultural societies.

References

Allemann-Ghionda, C. 2000. "Dewey in Post-war Italy: The Case of Re-education." *Studies in Philosophy and Education* 19 (1–2): 53–67.

Augelli, A., F. Gobbo, I. Pescarmona, and M. Traversi. 2005. *Cooperative learning nelle classi multiculturali. Uno sguardo all'istruzione complessa. Quaderni di formazione interculturale.* Bologna: CD/Lei.

Bandura, A. 1969. *Principles of Behaviour Modification.* New York: Holt, Rinehart & Winston.

CEC. 2000. *Presidency conclusions of the Lisbon European council, march 23/24.* Brussels: Commission of the European Communities. http://www.europarl.europa.eu/summits/lis1_en.htm

Chiosso, G. 1997. *Novecento Pedagogico.* Brescia: Editrice La Scuola.

Cohen, E. 1994. *Designing Groupwork: Strategies for Heterogeneous Classrooms.* New York: Teachers College Press.

Cohen, E. 1997. "Understanding Status Problems: Sources and Consequences." In *Working for Equity in Heterogeneous Classrooms. Socio-logical Theory in Practice*, edited by E. Cohen and R. Lotan, 61–76. New York: Teachers College Press.

Cohen, E., D. Briggs, N. Filby, E. Chin, M. Male, S. Mata, S. McBride, T. Perez, R. Quintar-Sarellana, and P. Swanson. 2004. "Teaching Demanding Strategies for Cooperative Learning: A Comparative Study of Five Teacher Education Programs." In *Teaching Cooperative Learning. The Challenge for Teacher Education*, edited by E. Cohen, C. M. Brody, and M. Sapon-Shevin, 143–165. Albany: State University of New York Press.

Cohen, E., and R. Lotan, eds. 1997a. *Working for Equity in Heterogeneous Classrooms. Socio-logical Theory in Practice.* New York: Teachers College Press.

Cohen, E., and R. Lotan. 1997b. "Raising Expectations for Competence: The Effectiveness of Status Interventions." In *Working for Equity in Heterogeneous Classrooms. Socio-logical Theory in Practice*, edited by E. Cohen and R. Lotan, 77–91. New York: Teachers College Press.

Cohen, E., and R. Lotan. 2004. "Equity in Heterogeneous Classrooms." In *Handbook of Research on Multicultural Education*, edited by J. A. Banks and A. M. C. Banks, 736–750. San Francisco: Jossey-Bass.

Ellis, N. E., and R. A. Lotan. 1997. "Teachers as Learners: Feedback, Conceptual Understanding, and Implementation." In *Working for Equity in Heterogeneous Classrooms. Sociological Theory in Practice*, edited by E. Cohen and R. Lotan, 209–222. New York: Teachers College Press.

Florio-Ruane, S. 1996. "La cultura e l'organizzazione sociale della classe scolastica." In *Antropologia dell'educazione*, edited by F. Gobbo, 171–190. Milan: Edizioni Unicopli.

Gardner, H. 1983. *Frames of Mind. The Theory of Multiple Intelligences*. New York: Basic Books.

Geertz, C. 1987. *Description: Toward an Interpretive Theory of Cultures*. New York: Basic Books.

Glaser, B. G., and A. L. Strauss. 1967. *The Discovery of Grounded Theory: Strategies for Qualitative Research*. Chicago: Aldine.

Gobbo, F. 2007. "Teaching Teachers Cooperative Learning." In *Social Justice and Intercultural Education: An Open-Ended Dialogue*, edited by G. Bhatti, 76–92. London: Trentham Books.

Gonon, P. 2000. "Education, Not Democracy?. The Apolitical Dewey." *Studies in Philosophy and Education* 19 (1–2): 141–157.

Hargreaves, A., and P. Woods, eds. 1984. *Classrooms & Staffrooms. The Sociology of Teachers and Teaching*. London: Open University Press.

High Level Group. 2004. *Facing the challenge. The Lisbon strategy for growth and employment. Report from the high level group chaired by Wim Kok*. Brussels: Commission of the European Communities. http://ec.europa.eu/research/evaluations/pdf/archive/fp6-evidence-base/evaluation_studies_and_reports/evaluation_studies_and_reports_2004/the_lisbon_strategy_for_growth_and_employment__report_from_the_high_level_group.pdf

Jeffrey, B., and G. Troman. 2006. "Time for Ethnography." In *Researching Education Policy: Ethnographic Experiences*, edited by G. Troman, B. Jeffrey, and D. Beach, 22–36. London: The Tufnell Press.

Mills, C. W. 1959. *The Sociological Imagination*. London: Oxford University Press.

Oelkers, J. 2000. "Democracy and Education: About the Future of a Problem." *Studies in Philosophy and Education* 19 (1–2): 3–19.

Perrenet, J., and J. Terwel. 1997. "Learning Together in Multicultural Groups: A Curriculum Innovation." *Curriculum and Teaching* 12 (1): 31–44.

Pescarmona, I. 2010. "Complex Instruction: Managing Professional Development and School Culture." *Intercultural Education* 21 (3): 219–227.

Pescarmona, I. 2011a. "Working on Cooperative Learning: Challenges in Implementing a New Strategy." *International Journal of Pedagogies and Learning* 6 (3): 167–174.

Pescarmona, I. 2011b. "Creativity and Competence in Experimenting Complex Instruction: From the Perspective of Pupils." *Experiments in Education* XXXIX (3): 81–90.

Pescarmona, I. 2012. *Innovazione educativa tra entusiasmo e fatica. Un'etnografia dell'apprendimento cooperativo*. Roma: CISU.

Pescarmona, I. 2014. "Learning to Participate Through Complex Instruction." *Intercultural Education* 25 (3): 187–196.

Phillips, D., and K. Ochs, eds. 2004. *Educational Policy Borrowing: Historical Perspectives*. Oxford Studies in Comparative Education. Oxford: Symposium Books.

Rosenholtz, S., and S. H. Rosenholtz. 1981. "Classroom Organization and the Perception of Ability." *Sociology of Education* 54 (2): 132–140.

Rosenthal, R., and L. Jacobson. 1972. *Pigmalione in classe. Aspettative degli insegnanti e sviluppo intellettuale degli allievi*. Milan: Franco Angeli editore.

Sansoè, R. 2007. "Figli dell'immigrazione: nati da famiglie immigrate e cresciuti nella scuola italiana." In *La ricerca per una scuola che cambia*, edited by F. Gobbo, 115–140. Padua: Imprimitur.

Simpson, C. 1981. "Classroom Structure and the Organization of Ability." *Sociology of Education* 54 (2): 120–132.

Steiner-Khamsi, G., ed. 2004. *The Global Politics of Educational Borrowing and Lending*. New York: Teachers College, Columbia University.

Sternberg, R. J., and L. Spear-Swerling. 1966. *Teaching for Thinking*. Washington, DC: American Psychological Association.

Troman, G., B. Jeffrey, and G. Walford, eds. 2004. *Identity, Agency and Social Institutions in Educational Ethnography*. Amsterdam: Elsevier.

Walford, G., ed. 2002. *Doing a Doctorate in Educational Ethnography*. Vol. 7. Oxford: Elsevier.

The Storyline approach: promoting learning through cooperation in the second language classroom

Sharon Ahlquist

School of Education and Environment, Kristianstad University, Kristianstad, Sweden

> In the Storyline approach, a fictive world is created in the classroom, with learners working in small groups, taking on the role of characters in a story. The story develops as they work on a range of tasks which integrate the practical and theoretical content of the curriculum. This article reports on a study based on the syllabus for English, in which a class of Swedish 11–13-year-olds took on the roles of families who had moved into a new street in England, and highlights the role played by cooperative group work in the second learning process.

Introduction

The Storyline approach originated in Scotland in the 1960s as a response to changes in the national primary curriculum. The introduction of *environmental studies* required an inter-disciplinary approach to teaching for which teachers in their training had not been prepared. Teacher educators working at Jordanhill College of Education, Glasgow, now part of the University of Strathclyde, subsequently developed the idea of using a narrative framework within which theoretical and practical subjects could be integrated. Originally known as *topic work*, the name *Storyline* was adopted during the 1980s. As a teacher educator at Kristianstad University in southern Sweden, I have worked with Storyline since 2000, incorporating it into initial teacher education programmes and in-service courses for the teaching of English as a second language (L2) at all levels of the school system.

In the Storyline approach, a fictive world is created in the classroom. Working in small groups, learners take on the roles of characters in a story and keep these roles throughout the Storyline topic, typically for four to six weeks. The story, set in a specific place and time, has a clear beginning, middle and end, usually concluding with some kind of celebration. The narrative unfolds as the learners work together on *key questions*. These open questions, based on curriculum content, structure and provide narrative impetus for the story in the same way as do chapters in a book. For instance, the key question *Who are you?* often starts the Storyline by establishing the *people*. The learners create a character individually, in agreement with their group; they make a stick puppet, papier maché doll or a drawing to represent the character, write about the character and introduce themselves in role as a group

LEARNING TO LEARN TOGETHER

to the rest of the class. A later question, heralding a development in the story, might be introduced following the receipt of a letter or the arrival of a 'visitor' (class teacher or a colleague), asking for help. Good key questions are a vital component in the Storyline approach; they incorporate subject content into the story in a meaningful way and thus motivate the learners to engage with it.

Storyline is underpinned by constructivist and social constructivist approaches to learning, as discussed in Falkenberg (2007). Learners construct their knowledge through working with the tasks, linking their acquired with existing knowledge. This process is facilitated as the learners interact in groups to complete their tasks. While group work in Storyline embodies the principles of cooperation, namely that learners have individual responsibility and are collectively responsible for completing a task, two things distinguish these groups from those formed during normal class work. One is that they work together for the duration of the Storyline (although they will also work in other group constellations, in pairs and individually); the second is that they, as a group, have something in common in the story, which potentially enhances the feeling of solidarity. For example, they might be members of a family who have moved into a street, with their neighbours being the other groups in the class.

Besides the nature of the group, another characteristic feature of the Storyline approach is the way in which the aesthetic subjects are integrated with the theoretical. For example, a frieze is used to display drawings, models and written work. The aim is to document the developing story, provide a graphic overview of where the learners are in the story and to show respect for their work by making it visible to all. It also allows the teacher to make a change to the display in order to anticipate future developments and so provoke interest.

It can be seen from the above brief description that the role of the teacher in the Storyline approach is quite different from that with which most classroom teachers are familiar and, perhaps, most comfortable, namely leading from the front. In Storyline, the teacher still leads, but less obviously. Having planned the Storyline topic based on curriculum content, preferably together with colleagues teaching classes in the same year group, and formulated stimulating key questions, the teacher's role is to introduce the topic, making sure that the learners know what they are going to be working with, for how long and why (i.e. the links to the curriculum). Once they have this information, the learners, with help, set themselves individual learning goals based on the curriculum content to be covered. The teacher will have used knowledge of the talents, proficiencies and personalities of the learners to create groups which can be expected to work effectively together, and will provide guidance, rather than answers, as the groups work on the key questions, keep the learners on track and provide regular opportunities for reviewing learning. It is sometimes said that in Storyline, the teacher provides the *line* and the learners the *content* of the story. Although the teacher knows where and when the story will end, what happens along the way as the learners respond to the key questions depends on the efforts of the learners. Looked at in this way, it can be seen that a successful Storyline topic is the result not only of a cooperative partnership between the learners themselves, but between the learners and their teacher.

Over the last 50 years, the Storyline approach has been adopted in many countries, being represented on almost every continent, and has been implemented at all levels of education from pre-school to university, as well as in nurse education and the business world. It flourishes in contexts where teachers have freer hands regarding materials and methods (Barr and Frame 2006). While most work has been within first language (L1) education, the benefits for second language (L2) education have become more widely understood. A Comenius-funded partnership (2003–2006) between teacher educators in Germany,

Finland, Poland and the UK (Ehlers et al. 2006) was the first project to link Storyline and foreign language teaching in primary schools, producing teaching materials, training teachers to use them and evaluating the impact of learning (increase in motivation and benefits for vocabulary acquisition).

It is difficult to say to what extent the approach is in use at any given time since this becomes known only when teachers present their work at an international Storyline conference, held every three years, on the international website (www.storyline-scotland.com/storyline-international), or one of the national websites (for instance, Sweden, Turkey and Slovenia). Somewhat surprisingly, there has been little scholarly research to date. Subjects which have been investigated in education are learner ownership (Hofmann 2008), pupil motivation in a primary class (Mitchell-Barrett 2010) and teacher motivation (Emo 2010); in health studies, Edith Mark (2009), working with Danish children suffering from eating disorders, created a story and fictive characters with the children as a way of approaching the problem.

Although there is a lack of research into the uses and effects of Storyline, there is anecdotal evidence in the school world both from teachers and student teachers who have worked with the approach. There are a number of common themes. For example, teachers report on how practical work helps learners grasp abstract concepts and on how providing expertise to the group or the class when in role raises the status of learners whose opinions are otherwise often ignored. One word which recurs in the description of the Storyline experiences of learners of all ages is 'fun'. This is significant: John Hattie's (2009) extensive examination of factors which contribute to effective learning found that where there was enjoyment, achievement was higher.

In this article, I will present and discuss the findings of a study into the impact on the learning of English in a class of Swedish learners aged 11–13, beginning with an overview of the literature regarding young language learners, which provides theoretical support for an interdisciplinary approach, narrative framework and the use of cooperative group work. The study was not cited in a framework of cooperative learning, but many tasks, such as jigsaw and information gap, are recognisable from this approach, and the principles of cooperative learning (individual accountability, collective responsibility, face-to-face interaction and small group social skills) are integral to successful Storyline work.

Young language learners

For many young learners, English is introduced as a foreign language at school. The age at which this happens varies from country to country, with six to seven being usual. The number and length of lessons per week also varies, with perhaps less than an hour in total for the youngest pupils and 3 or 4 lessons of about 45 minutes for older primary age children. Young children generally approach English lessons positively. They learn holistically, with their whole bodies and through their emotions, responding well to stories, songs, games, movement, drama and thematic work, all of which are considered to promote language acquisition. Drama, for example, can reduce tension (Allström 2010), and it promotes learning by providing a context in which learners have to communicate with each other. However, as children become older, motivation, which is necessary for effective learning (Dörnyei 2009), becomes less stable (Lantolf and Thorne 2006) and initial positive attitudes have been found to decline from as early as the age of 10–11 (Enever 2011). Since the primary years lay the foundations for positive attitudes as learners progress through their education (Cameron 2001; Nikolov 2001), this is of serious concern to teachers.

LEARNING TO LEARN TOGETHER

Some reasons for loss of motivation at this time have been identified. As learners approach puberty, they become self-conscious. The very activities which foster language acquisition in young learners become a source of embarrassment (singing, for example). The opinions of friends are important at this stage in life, as is the need for a positive self-image, which owes much to the view of one's peers. A fear of making mistakes, being laughed at by others and publicly corrected by the teacher can create reluctance to speak English. If forced to do so, or from the fear of being forced to do so, learners can become anxious, which causes them to under-perform (Krashen 1982; Alanen 2003; Moon 2005; Mihaljevic Djigunovic 2009; Lundberg 2010). At the same time, the need to feel a sense of progress increases; the extent to which the learners feel they are progressing, or not, impacts on their motivation. A negative self-image as a language learner can result in poor motivation and a negative effect on learning (Skolverket 2004).

Cognitively, young learners are in a state of development, with those in the age bracket 10–13 making the transition from holistic learning to the more analytical, though far from all have developed analytically by the time they start secondary education (Malmberg 2000). Learners in this age group express a preference for ways of working which utilise all their senses (Warrington and Younger 2006). This is an interesting finding since it reflects the view of Gardner (2004) that a multi-sensory approach allows 'different kinds of minds' (11) to engage with and to learn curriculum content in different ways. However, in the later years of primary education, in Sweden at least, teachers often rely heavily on textbooks (Skolinspektionen 2010). Particularly in cases where the teacher lacks formal training in the teaching of English, this may lead to a focus on grammar teaching for which many learners are cognitively unready. The use of unsuitable classroom methodology has been identified as another reason for loss of motivation (Nikolov 2009).

With late primary age learners, a combination of tasks which prioritise meaning, involve holistic use of the language skills and which direct the learners' attention to the linguistic forms which convey meaning is considered to work best (Lightbown and Spada 2013). Over the last 30 years, second language education has seen a considerable and sustained research interest in task-based education. Though there are many definitions, task-based learning and teaching (TBLT) is considered to involve meaningful use of language in a specific context with a tangible outcome (Ellis 2003; Nunan 2004; Samuda and Bygate 2008) and can involve learners working individually, in pairs or in groups. Often in a task, there is a gap between what individual learners know, and they have to cooperate to bridge the gap (for more information about such tasks, see McCafferty, Jacobs, and DaSilva Iddings 2006). One example might be that the learners have to find a time to meet. Each learner writes a schedule of their activities for a given week. They then speak to a partner or partners in an attempt to find a date on which they can meet. The language structures in focus here are the statement and question forms of the continuous present: *What are you doing on Monday evening? I'm going to the cinema.*

Tasks might also include practical work: for example, learners working in small groups represent tourist offices from the different regions of their country and are to present their region at an international fair. Such a task can include the learners' own drawings and information technology in a number of ways. There are both cognitive and affective benefits. Firstly, learners benefit mostly from a display when they have been involved in making it (Moon 2005). Secondly, as Crandall (1999) argues, the use of practical work allows learners to be seen in a more multidimensional way by their peers. The significance of this can be seen in research into cooperative learning (Cohen, Lotan, and Holthius 1995), where lack of learner participation, which plays a key role in learning, can often be attributed to the negative attitudes and rebuttals of other group members. Learners who have low

39

proficiency in the theoretical subjects may have an artistic talent. Valuing and utilising this talent in the language classroom are likely to have a positive effect on the individual learner's self-image and their approach to English, leading to greater participation and more effective learning. In fact, the benefits go beyond this. As Toohey (2000) points out, teachers also have assumptions about their learners, which can become established as fact if the learners have no opportunity to display a range of talents and facets of personality.

The use of group work in second language education, even with young learners whose language skills are under development, is supported by the research literature (Williams and Burden 1996; Cameron 2001; Moon 2005; Pinter 2005, 2006, 2007). Pair and group work allow more learners to speak at the same time than is the case in a traditional class, where the teacher asks a question and one learner at a time responds, and to speak beyond sentence level, so practising linking words. A pair/group format encourages those who are shy, or less secure, to use the language. Additionally, there is the issue of promoting mutual respect, as discussed above, by using everyone's strengths. Donato (2004) argues that the group's collective result is greater than that which can be achieved by individuals working on their own. However, this assumes that the proficiency levels within the group are similar (Watanabe and Swain 2007), or that the learners' knowledge areas complement each other – in other words, that the individuals respect and value each other's competence. Whether or not they do this depends very much on personality, which is the variable considered to have most influence on the effectiveness of group work (Klingner and Vaughn 2000; Storch 2001). For example, boys of all ages have been shown to attempt to dominate group work (Mercer and Littleton 2007); fear of failure may cause boys especially to disrupt the group's work (Warrington and Younger 2006); some children of both sexes prefer to work alone. One of the key elements in successful cooperative group work is social skills. Children are not born with these skills; they are learnt over time, through interaction and with guidance (Fisher 2005). Hence, pre-task modelling in a collaborative task, where the teacher demonstrates for the partners what they are supposed to do, leads to more effective work on task on the one hand and promotes a more harmonious dynamic on the other (Kim and McDonough 2011).

Where learners are willing to help each other and willing to be helped, both have the potential to develop within the Zone of Proximal Development (ZPD) (Vygotsky 1978). In second language acquisition, the ZPD is defined as 'the difference between the L2 learner's developmental level as determined by independent language use and the higher level of potential development as determined by how language is used in collaboration with a more capable interlocutor' (Ohta 1995, 249). The *more capable interlocutor* refers not just to a teacher, but can be a peer. Interestingly, Wells (1999) uses a broader definition of the ZPD – an interactive space in which individual identities can be transformed in numerous and unpredictable ways. This encompasses not only the possibility of cognitive development through group interaction, but highlights potential affective benefits. As was discussed earlier, a positive self-image is a necessary ingredient in successful L2 acquisition as learners approach puberty.

Significantly, it can also be added that, even where some of the interaction has been in the L1, it has been found to have a positive impact on young learners' development in speaking English (Enever, 2011). This finding is supported by previous research, which has identified the following as important roles for the L1 in the second language classroom: it allows the learners to talk about and manage the task (Van Lier 2004; Storch and Aldosari 2010), stay on task (Platt and Brooks 1994), talk about the L2 (Lantolf and Thorne 2006), express identity (Carless 2007; Fuller 2009) and manage their relationships (Swain and

Lapkin 2000). In short, it allows everyone to be involved, which is important for the smooth functioning of the group and consequently for the learning of all concerned.

The Storyline approach can be considered as a specific form of TBLT (Kocher 2006; Kirsch 2008; Ahlquist 2013). Tasks drive the story and add detail to it. They may target particular grammatical structures, either to introduce new structures or to consolidate existing knowledge, and are designed to practise language functions as stipulated in a national syllabus for English. For instance, in Sweden, learners aged 7–9 should, among other things, be able to give a simple oral presentation of themselves. In the 10–13 age range, they should be able to participate in simple conversations. This includes the strategic use of questions, politeness phrases and small talk. Tasks also incorporate new vocabulary – the vocabulary of the topic, which can be recycled in different, but natural ways, throughout the Storyline. This is significant for two, connected, reasons. Firstly, research into vocabulary acquisition highlights the need for recycling (Read 2007); secondly, learners of all ages often judge their progress in terms of the number of words they know. In teaching based on textbooks, or that which is task-based but without a common theme over a range of tasks, recycling does not occur, to the detriment of learning.

Storyline is also characterised by the narrative framework within which all tasks are carried out. The story develops, often unpredictably, stimulating the imagination of the learners. As Egan (1988) and others have made clear, the imagination is a powerful learning tool and one that is underused in the traditional classroom beyond the early primary years. The tasks are meaningful within the context of the story and provide practice of the language skills in ways that are motivational. For example, while boys are considered to be more reluctant writers of fiction than girls, a Storyline topic offers a range of possible writing genres, from emails to reports, which may appeal more to boys. Some of these writing tasks will be the result of group cooperation. While writing is a source of anxiety for many (Griva, Tsakiridou, and Nihoritou 2009), a collaborative effort has the potential to reduce that anxiety. Even when the work is individual, where the learners are sitting face to face, they are able to ask for and provide help within the group. Under these conditions, where learners either collaborate or help each other on individual tasks, there is a sense of solidarity, heightened by the nature of the Storyline group (being a member of a family, for example), not just within the group, but within the class. Together, the learners experience what Bruner calls a 'shared narrative' (2002, 15). This has implications for the relationships between the learners and their learning. As Allwright (2003) and Nikolov (2009) have argued, the quality of work produced in a classroom is highly dependent on the atmosphere of that classroom.

The impact of the Storyline approach on the young language learner classroom

In light of the established research link between enjoyment, motivation and achievement, I investigated the language development in a class of 11–13-year-olds over the course of a Storyline topic. The research questions were the following:

(1) To what features of the *Storyline* topic do the learners respond more positively?
(2) To what features of the *Storyline* topic do the learners respond less positively?
(3) What changes in language use can be observed during the *Storyline*?
(4) How do the learners mediate the task requirements for each other and to what extent do they use tools to mediate the tasks?
(5) What and how do the learners think they learn through working with the *Storyline* topic?

LEARNING TO LEARN TOGETHER

The conceptual framework for this case study was sociocultural theory, which is concerned with *change*. Gaining ground in the field of research into second language acquisition, a sociocultural perspective makes no distinction between language *use* and language *acquisition*: learners acquire language as they use it, a process in which interaction plays a key role (Firth and Wagner 2007). Moreover, the socio-affective context, which includes relationships between the learners, is considered to influence the learning process (Atkinson 2002; Lantolf 2005). It is this emphasis on the importance of social and affective factors which distinguishes the sociocultural perspective on second language acquisition from the purely cognitive, which has hitherto dominated the field (Kasper 1997; Long 1997; Gass 1998).

The subjects of the study were 1 class of 32 children aged 11–13, working with 2 teachers. Both the children and their teachers had previously worked with Storyline topics in Swedish and in English. The study lasted for five weeks, during which time the children worked with their Storyline four days a week and for about two hours each day. The topic was *Our Sustainable Street*, in which the learners, working in groups of four, took on the roles of families who had just moved into a newly built street in a fictive English town. As the story developed, they took part in a project to live in a more sustainable way, had to contend with the problem of outsiders dumping rubbish on land adjacent to their street and to deal with the arrival of anti-social neighbours. As well as being based on the syllabus for English, this Storyline topic also integrated learning objectives from art, social and natural science. The aim was to consolidate the grammatical structures and vocabulary which the learners had worked with since starting English at the age of seven, as well as to introduce vocabulary to do with sustainable development (*climate change, pollution, global warming* and *carbon footprint*, for instance). The study was not an attempt to teach these concepts; they had already been covered in Swedish prior to starting the Storyline.

The following key questions structured the topic:

(1) Who are you?
(2) What is your house like?
(3) What can you do to help the climate?
(4) What can we do about the dumping in our street?
(5) What can we do about the problems with our neighbours?

I shall go on to explain in some detail how the learners worked both individually and cooperatively in the third key question. Briefly, in the other key questions, they worked as follows: in the first question, the learners created the characters, as outlined at the beginning of this article; in the second, they drew their house and wrote an estate agent's description; in the fourth, they wrote a letter of complaint to the local council about the waste ground and were invited to design a new park to be situated on the land. In the last question, they explored the problems of anti-social neighbours (with one of the teachers playing the part of the mother of the family and being interviewed by her 'neighbours'). The Storyline came to a close with a street party at which games were played, making use of the topical and lexical content of the story, and food was prepared following English recipes.

In Key Question 3, the families received a letter inviting them to think about their impact on the climate and to take part in a project to live in a more sustainable way. The letter invited them to a meeting at the town hall, during which they listened to a lecture given by one of the teachers in role as an expert on climate change (for more on the drama technique *teacher-in-role*, see Heathcote and Bolton 1996). Before attending the

LEARNING TO LEARN TOGETHER

meeting, each learner, in role, wrote a diary of a typical day. After the lecture, and after answering in their groups a short quiz, the answers to which were provided in a written summary of the lecture, they individually reviewed their daily activities to find ways in which they impacted negatively on the climate. The class was then divided into new groups, based on the age of the characters, and their task was to prepare a collage in words and pictures showing their group's impact on the climate. The aim was to provide different perspectives on the subject, based on the ages of the characters. This task is similar to Group Investigation (Sharan and Sharan 1992) in cooperative learning. In the next stage, using a variation of another cooperative learning technique, *two stay, two stray*, one learner remained with the collage to present it and answer questions, while the rest of the group visited the collages of the other groups. The aim here was to be able to compare what their own group had done with the results of the other groups.

Within this key question, there are a number of distinct tasks, all of which are meaningful within the story and which develop it by adding detail to the characters' lives within the context of real-world concerns. Individual tasks preceded group tasks in order to ensure that everyone had the means to contribute to the group effort, producing, presenting/asking about others' collage. Thus, in terms of the language skills, the learners read the letter informing them about the project and the meeting, and also the summary of the lecture. They wrote individual diaries, which focused on the simple present tense, vocabulary of daily life and cultural content concerning life in an English-speaking country, and analysed it for negative climate impact. They listened to the lecturer and to the other group presenters. As regards speaking, they spoke while creating the collage, discussing vocabulary and grammar; they also spoke when they presented their own collage or asked questions about those of the others.

What can be seen here is the way in which face-to-face interaction has the potential to facilitate language learning: firstly, it feels natural and that in itself may prompt a desire to speak – in many language classrooms the learners sit in rows talking to the back of each other's heads; secondly, the need to communicate is inbuilt in the task, meaning that the learners want to listen to and ask questions of each other in order to complete their task; thirdly, they are physically grouped around the collage, possibly standing and free to move, which might reduce tension. Even if they lapsed into the L1 as they discussed the collage (which was the case), the focus of the writing was the L2 and discussions concerned which form of a verb to use, what the English words were for certain objects or how words were spelt.

This was a qualitative study, which used the following sources of data: observation notes, learner journals, questionnaire, interviews with learners and teachers, copies of the learners' texts and some video recording. The aim was to capture as full a picture as possible of what was happening in the classroom and in the children's learning. Although I took no part in the teaching, I was present in the classroom on all occasions, positioning myself near different groups at different times, noting down significant words and phrases, as well as the metalinguistic behaviour of the learners. During the pilot study, I had filmed different groups as they worked. This proved unsatisfactory for two reasons. One concerned the noise level in the class, the other that the camera clearly influenced behaviour, with the learners either speaking very quietly or turning towards the camera. After the main study had ended, I recorded groups at work on a task which could have been used in the story, in a separate room, with the purpose of illustrating how learners can interact during a Storyline task.

Once a week, the learners reflected on what they had learnt, responding in their journals to questions from the teachers. At the end of the Storyline, they completed a questionnaire in which they listed their favourite five features (not ranked), stated what they had liked best, not liked and how Storyline had helped them to learn English. A representative sample of boys and girls, older and younger, was interviewed individually to follow up the questionnaires (for instance, if the learner's favourite feature had been the artwork, I wanted to know how this could help them learn English or if it was just for fun). In the case of the teachers, they received in advance of the interview a list of questions concerning the language development of the learners, how well the groups had functioned and whether this way of working suited everyone. All data were collected in Swedish. Finally, by comparing writing done at the beginning, in the middle and the end of the Storyline, I attempted to identify signs of learning development with regard to grammar, vocabulary or syntax. Full details concerning data collection and analysis can be found in Ahlquist (2011).

The findings and discussion

In this section, I will discuss the collected findings. Briefly, in order to synthesise the findings, each data set was analysed in relation to the research questions, with colour coding used to highlight the different aspects. For example, the observation notes were coded POS, NPOS, LANG and MED to refer to learners' positive/less positive responses to tasks, their use of English and the way in which they helped each other, including use of the L1. In analysing the journals, I looked for learner attitudes to their work, what they thought they had learnt and how they had developed in the language skills. Extracts from the data are here written in italics.

Table 1 shows the relative popularity of the Storyline features.

The two most popular features were *artwork* and working in a *group*. The high ranking of *group work* contrasts with the unpopularity of *working alone*. This highlights the appeal of working together with others in the Storyline. However, while *imagination* is rated highly, working with a *made up story* is not. One explanation might be that the item was not understood by the learners, or, perhaps more likely, that the story in itself is of less importance than the character over which the individual learner has more creative control.

Table 2 shows that there were some differences between the preferences of boys and girls. The *group* was more important to the girls, as was using *imagination*. Comments

Table 1. The number of learners who placed each *Storyline* feature in their top five.

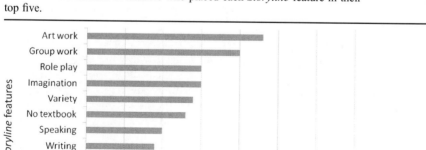

LEARNING TO LEARN TOGETHER

Table 2. The number of boys and girls, respectively, who included each *Storyline* feature in their top 5.

Features	Boys (13)	Girls (18)	Total (31)
Artwork	11	12	23 (74%)
Group	7	13	20 (65%)
Role play	8	7	15 (48%)
Imagination	3	12	15 (48%)
Variety	7	7	14 (45%)
No textbook	9	4	13 (42%)
Speaking	6	4	10 (32%)
Writing	2	7	9 (29%)
Reading	2	7	9 (29%)
Working alone	4	3	7 (23%)
Made up story	2	3	5 (16%)
Diary	1	4	5 (16%)

about their favourite part of Storyline were, for example, *having a family, drawing and writing because you are that person then*. For the boys, not using a textbook was a popular feature.

Potentially, there are lessons to be taken here for the teaching of English in non-Storyline classes, that is, in the more traditional classroom. Based on this study, it can be said that the integration of practical work with language teaching, the extensive use of cooperative group work and the use of a varied range of tasks which encourage the learners to be creative can have a positive effect on language learning since this fosters conditions in which learning becomes enjoyable (or as the children in the study expressed it, Storyline is 'fun').

However, if Storyline is to be more than 'fun', there must be evidence of language change. Based on classroom observations, teacher interviews, analysis of the learners' texts, and not least the questionnaires, journals and interviews of the learners themselves, learning gains could be ascertained in a number of areas. Firstly, with regard to the spoken language, over time there was less anxiety about speaking English and therefore less reluctance to do so. The importance of this finding cannot be overstated. As was discussed in regard to the research literature on second language acquisition, anxiety is an impediment to learning as fear of speaking the language, or of being called upon to do so, causes the learner to under-perform. Reduced anxiety leads to greater willingness to speak, thus opening up opportunities for acquisition. As was stated earlier, the theoretical framework for the study was sociocultural theory, in which learners are considered to acquire the language as they use it.

With regard to listening, not only were the learners themselves aware of finding this easier over time, it was apparent in the classroom. At the beginning of the study, the teachers would almost always have to supplement instructions in English with a Swedish translation, or face many questions from their confused pupils. From the beginning of the third week, it was clear that the children understood the instructions from the way in which they approached their tasks. Any uncertainty was dealt with in the group. In response to the question regarding why they thought they had improved in the productive skills, the answers for speaking and listening were similar: *we did a lot of it, we had to do it* and, in the case of listening, *it was important information*.

Although some children evaluated an improvement in their reading skills, others did not. This is based not only on the children's expressed views in their journals, but in a comparison between the data of two Likert scales. Before the study began, the children completed a questionnaire regarding the kinds of activities they liked in English, whether they used it in their leisure time and a four-point Likert scale on which they assessed their current performance in the language skills. They were asked to rate their skills again on the questionnaire they completed at the end of the Storyline. For reading in particular, the ratings immediately after the Storyline were lower than those before it. One explanation might be that the reading texts which the learners worked with in their textbooks were easier than those they encountered in the Storyline, many of which featured the core vocabulary of the topic, namely sustainable development. It may be that if the learners had assessed their reading on the Likert scale once they had returned to their textbook, the rating would have been higher. This step will be incorporated into future studies.

With regard to writing, the teachers' view was that they had *never seen so much freely produced text*. Analysis of the texts – a character description, an email to a friend and a longer letter – revealed attempts to use structures which had been recently taught, or not yet taught, in the case of the younger learners. One such example is the relative clause. Other examples are the incorporation of new words. The learners themselves were aware of learning more words, which is important motivationally, becoming surer of spellings and of word order. In the teachers' view, the reason for this was that *they have lived with these words*.

The popular features of Storyline and the language developments have been addressed; what remains is the important question of the role in learning played by mediation in three respects: classroom resources, the first language and group work. With regard to classroom resources such as dictionaries and reference books, it can be said that although there was greater willingness over time to consult these resources, use of a dictionary remained the last, rather than first, resort for some learners, although more willingness was displayed when the word search could be done on the class computer. The probable reason for this is the poor dictionary skills of some learners. The use of online dictionaries, into which the unknown word can be typed directly, makes the search easier and therefore less laborious.

The use of the L1 was seen to serve the purposes identified in the research literature, namely that it allowed everyone to be involved, to discuss the L2 and to keep the task on track. In other words, it facilitated the group work which lies at the heart of the Storyline approach. The teachers did their best to construct groups that could be expected to function well, taking into account a balance of the sexes, ages, talents and personalities. This was not an easy task and some groups functioned less well for reasons that could not have been predicted. Nevertheless, though some groups found it harder to cooperate due to personality conflicts, group work was the second most popular aspect of this study, suggesting that the benefits, as far as the learners were concerned, outweighed the drawbacks. Reasons for liking group work, especially among the less proficient boys, were (with regard to writing) that *you can get help; you can ask if you don't understand; it's more fun*. Where there were clashes in the groups, resulting in a lack of democratic decision-making and fair distribution of work, the respective group's work was less positively evaluated by the individuals. Such clashes were most often caused by the attempts of some to dominate, or because all the learners wanted to do the drawing where there was only one per family (such as the family car, the details of which had been agreed on by the group).

Nevertheless, what emerges from the data is a sense of solidarity: *I didn't draw but I helped decide; everybody helped; it was good in the family*. This last point highlights the affective benefits of Storyline – the nature of the group. In this case it was family. 'Bye, sister' was overheard as one group member temporarily left the group to join another constellation. It was this group which consistently rehearsed its presentations for the benefit of the least proficient member, practising what she had to say so that she would be able to contribute equally in front of the class – an example of cooperation where the success of all collectively depends on the success of the individual.

Although not all groups consciously supported their less proficient members in this way, the on-task cooperation between the individuals in the groups proved, in the opinion of the teachers, to benefit two types of learner in particular: the less proficient persevered where they would have given up when working alone, and the more proficient of the younger pupils benefited from the competence of the older children and were, according to the teachers, *pushed to perform*. In other words, within the group, conditions were created for development within the ZPD. While the teachers did not comment on the benefits here for the most proficient, it can be suggested, in line with Vygotsky, that their knowledge was consolidated as they helped their peers. What the teachers did see as an advantage for the most proficient was that the Storyline topic of sustainability gave them a challenge they so rarely get otherwise, where the teacher's attention is, of necessity, directed towards the least proficient. This is a problem in countries such as Sweden where all abilities are taught together. However, differentiated learning is possible in a Storyline topic. For instance, in Key Question 3, the less proficient may write a shorter diary. This still enables them to bring suggestions to the group for inclusion in the collage.

Conclusion

Storyline offers an approach to teaching which incorporates features children like – art, using their imagination, role play and variety. It can exist alongside a textbook on which the class's work is normally based. For example, topics such as family and daily life can be explored in a Storyline at a simple level; the same is true of subjects such as sports, popular culture or history, which feature in secondary level textbooks. One of Storyline's most powerful components is the small group, working together on meaningful tasks, contributing to a developing story in which all have a stake. Learners in the study reported *looking forward* to coming to school and working with the story, wondering what will happen next because *there is always something new*. Within this framework, relationships build, both between the learners and the characters and between the learners themselves. The bond within a well-functioning group is a strong and supportive one, and almost as strong are the bonds within the class as they share the developing narrative. This has powerful implications for the atmosphere in the classroom, which the research literature highlights as an important factor in the quality of the learning which occurs there. This is aptly illustrated by the words of a shy, less proficient, younger pupil, who summed up her development during the Storyline work with these words: *I dare to speak more now because nobody laughs at me when I get it wrong. They didn't before either, but now I know.*

As stated at the outset, this study was not conducted in a cooperative learning framework, but the principles and practices of the latter are inherent in Storyline. The effects on learning of more explicitly embedding the powerful tools of cooperative learning in a narrative framework, which engages both cognition and affect, are worthy of investigation.

References

Ahlquist, S. 2011. "The Impact of the Storyline Approach on the Young Language Learner Classroom." Doctoral thesis, University of Leicester.

Ahlquist, S. 2013. "'Storyline': A Task-Based Approach for the Young Learner Classroom." *ELT Journal* 67 (1): 41–51.

Alanen, R. 2003. "A Sociocultural Approach to Young Language Learners' Beliefs about Language Learning." In *Beliefs about SLA: New Research Approaches*, edited by P. Kalaja and A. M. F. Barcelos, 55–85. Dordrecht: Kluwer Academic Publishers.

Allström, M. 2010. "Drama som Metod i Engelska." In *Engelska för Yngre Åldrar*, edited by M. Estling Vannestål, and G. Lundberg, 113–128. Lund: Studentlitteratur (Using Drama to Teach English, *English for the Younger Years*).

Allwright, D. 2003. "Exploratory Practice: Rethinking Practitioner Research in Language Teaching." *Language Teaching Research* 7 (2): 113–141.

Atkinson, D. 2002. "Toward a Sociocognitive Approach to Second Language Acquisition." *The Modern Language Journal* 86 (iv): 25–45.

Barr, I., and B. Frame. 2006. "Implementing Storyline: The Professional Challenge." In *Beyond Storyline: Features, Principles and Pedagogical Profundity*, edited by J. Letschert, B. Grabbe-Letschert, and J. Greven, 49–57. Enschede: SLO, Netherlands Institute for Curriculum Development.

Bruner, J. 2002. *Making Stories: Law, Literature, Life*. Cambridge, MA: Harvard University Press.

Cameron, L. 2001. *Teaching Languages to Young Learners*. Cambridge: Cambridge University Press.

Carless, D. 2007. "Student Use of the Mother Tongue in the Task-Based Classroom." *ELT Journal* 62 (4): 331–338.

Cohen, E. G., R. A. Lotan, and N. Holthius. 1995. "Talking and Working Together: Conditions for Learning in Complex Instruction." In *Restructuring Schools: Promising Practices and Policies*, edited by M. T. Hallinan, 157–174. New York: Plenum Press.

Crandall, J. 1999. "Cooperative Language Learning and Affective Factors." In *Affect in Language Learning*, edited by J. Arnold, 226–245. Cambridge: Cambridge University Press.

Donato, R. 2004. "Aspects of Collaboration in Pedagogical Discourse." *Annual Review of Applied Linguistics* 24 (March): 284–302.

Dörnyei, Z. 2009. *The Psychology of Second Language Acquisition*. Oxford: Oxford University Press.

Egan, K. 1988. *Teaching as Storytelling: An Alternative Approach to Teaching and the Curriculum*. London: Routledge.

Ehlers, G., H. M. Järvinen, V. Brandford, and M. Materniak. 2006. *The Storyline Approach in the Foreign Language Classroom*. Comenius Project, 112381-CP-1-2003-1-DE-COMENIUS-21, 2003-2006.

Ellis, R. 2003. *Task-Based Language Learning and Teaching*. Oxford: Oxford University Press.

Emo, W. 2010. "Teachers Who Initiate Curriculum Innovation: Motivations and Benefits." Doctoral thesis, University of York.

Enever, J, ed. 2011. *Early Language Learning in Europe (ELLiE)*. London: British Council.

Falkenberg, C. 2007. "Learning Theory: Substantiating the Storyline Approach to Teaching." In *Storyline: Past, Present and Future*, edited by S. Bell, S. Harkness, and G. White, 43–53. Glasgow: University of Strathclyde Press.

Firth, A. and J. Wagner. 2007. "Second/Foreign Language Learning as a Social Accomplishment: Elaborations on a Reconceptualized SLA." *The Modern Language Journal* 91 (Focus Issue): 800–819.

Fisher, R. 2005. *Teaching Children to Think*. 2nd ed. Cheltenham: Nelson Thornes.

Fuller, J. M. 2009. "How Bilingual Children Talk: Strategic Codeswitching Among Children in Dual Language Programs." In *First Language Use in Second and Foreign Language Learning*, edited by M. Turnbull and J. Dailey-O'Cain, 115–130. Bristol: Multilingual Matters.

Gardner, H. 2004. *The Unschooled Mind: How Children Think and How Schools Should Teach* (10th Anniversary ed.). New York: Basic Books.

Gass, S. 1998. "Apples and Oranges: Or Why Apples Are Not Oranges and Don't Need To Be. A Response to Firth and Wagner." *Modern Language Journal* 82 (1): 83–90.

Griva, E., H. Tsakiridou, and I. Nihoritou. 2009. "A Study of FL Composing Process and Writing Strategies Employed by Young Learners." In *Early Learning of Modern Foreign Languages: Processes and Outcomes*, edited by M. Nikolov, 132–148. Bristol: Multilingual Matters.

Hattie, J. 2009. *Visible Learning: A Synthesis of over 800 Meta-Analyses Relating to Achievement*. Abingdon: Routledge.

Heathcote, D., and G. Bolton. 1996. *Drama for Learning*. Abingdon: Heinemann.

LEARNING TO LEARN TOGETHER

Hofmann, R. 2008. "Ownership and Alienation in Learning: A Socio-Cultural Perspective on the Construction and Learner Experiences of Agency in School." Doctoral thesis, University of Cambridge.

Kasper, G. 1997. "A Stands for Acquisition: A Response to Firth and Wagner." *Modern Language Journal* 81 (3): 307–312.

Kim, Y., and K. McDonough. 2011. "Using Pretask Modelling to Encourage Collaborative Learning Opportunities." *Language Teaching Research* 15 (2): 183–199.

Kirsch, C. 2008. *Teaching Foreign Languages in the Primary School*. London: Continuum.

Klingner, J. K., and S. Vaughn. 2000. "The Helping Behaviors of Fifth Graders While Using Collaborative Strategic Reading During ESL Content Classes." *TESOL Quarterly* 34 (1): 69–98.

Kocher, D. 2006. "Lernprozesse Anleiten, Unterstuetzen und Auswerten." *Der Fremdsprachlige Unterrrich/Englisch* 84: 18–21 [The Learning Process: Guiding, Supporting and Utilizing, The Foreign Language Lesson/English].

Krashen, S. 1982. *Principles and Practice in Second Language Acquisition*. Oxford: Pergamon.

Lantolf, J. P. 2005. "Sociocultural and Second Language Learning Research: An Exegesis." In *Handbook of Research in Second Language Teaching and Learning*, edited by E. Hinkel, 335–354. Mahwah, NJ: Erlbaum.

Lantolf, J. P., and S. Thorne. 2006. *Sociocultural Theory and the Genesis of Second Language Development*. Oxford: Oxford University Press.

Lightbown, P., and N. Spada. 2013. *How Languages Are Learned*. 4th ed. Oxford: Oxford University Press.

Long, M. H. 1997. "Construct Validity in SLA Research: A Response to Firth and Wagner." *Modern Languages Journal* 81 (3): 318–323.

Lundberg, G. 2010. "Perspektiv på Tidigt Engelsklärande." In *Engelska för Yngre Åldrar*, edited by M. Estling Vannestål and G. Lundberg, 15–34. Lund: Studentlitteratur [Perspective on an Early Start. English for the Younger Years].

Malmberg, P. ed. 2000. *I Huvudet på en Elev: Projektet STRIMS (Strategier vid Inlärning av Moderna Språk)*. Stockholm: Bonniers Utbildning AB [Inside a Pupil's Head: STRIMS Project, Strategies for Learning Modern Languages].

Mark, E. 2009. "Restriktiv Spisning i Narrative Belysning: En Faemonemologisk Undersögelse af Börns Oplevelser af Spisning ved Diabetes eller Overvaegt" [Restrictive Eating in a Narrative Light: A Phenomological Study of Diabetic or Overweight Children's Experiences with Eating]. Doctoral thesis, University of Aalborg.

McCafferty, S. G., G. M. Jacobs, and A. C. DaSilva Iddings. 2006. *Cooperative Learning and Second Language Teaching*. Cambridge: Cambridge University Press.

Mercer, N., and K. Littleton. 2007. *Dialogue and the Development of Children's Thinking: A Sociocultural Perspective*. Abingdon: Routledge.

Mihaljevic Djigunovic, J. 2009. "Impact of Learning Conditions on Young FL Learners' Motivation." In *Early Learning of Modern Foreign Languages: Processes and Outcomes*, edited by M. Nikolov, 75–89. Bristol: Multilingual Matters.

Mitchell-Barrett, R. 2010. "An Analysis of the Storyline Method in Primary School; Its Theoretical Underpinnings and Its Impact on Pupils' Intrinsic Motivation." Doctoral thesis, University of Durham.

Moon, J. 2005. *Children Learning English: A Guidebook for English Language Teachers*. Oxford: Macmillan.

Nikolov, M. 2001. "A Study of Unsuccessful Language Learners." In *Motivation and Second Language Acquisition*, edited by Z. Dörnyei and R. Schmidt, 149–169. Honolulu: University of Hawaii Press.

Nikolov, M. 2009. "Early Modern Foreign Language Programmes and Outcomes: Factors Contributing to Hungarian Learners' Proficiency." In *Early Learning of Modern Foreign Languages: Processes and Outcomes*, edited by M. Nikolov, 90–107. Bristol: Multilingual Matters.

Nunan, D. 2004. *Task-Based Language Teaching*. Cambridge: Cambridge University Press.

Ohta, A. S. 1995. "Applying Sociocultural Theory to an Analysis of Learner Discourse: Learner-Learner Collaborative Interaction in the Zone of Proximal Development." *Issues in Applied Linguistics* 6 (2): 93–122.

LEARNING TO LEARN TOGETHER

Pinter, A. 2005. "Task Repetition with 10-Year-Old Children." In *Teachers Exploring Tasks in English Language Teaching*, edited by C. Edwards and J. Willis, 113–126. Basingstoke: Macmillan Palgrave.

Pinter, A. 2006. *Teaching Young Language Learners*. Oxford: Oxford University Press.

Pinter, A. 2007. "Some Benefits of Peer–Peer Interaction: 10-Year-Old Children Practising with a Communicative Task." *Language Teaching Research* 11 (2): 189–207.

Platt, E., and F. B. Brooks. 1994. "The Acquisition Rich Environment Revisited." *The Modern Language Journal* 78 (4): 497–511.

Read, C. 2007. *500 Activities for the Primary Classroom*. Oxford: Macmillan.

Samuda, V., and M. Bygate. 2008. *Tasks in Second Language Learning*. London: Palgrave.

Sharan, Y., and S. Sharan. 1992. *Expanding Cooperative Learning Through Group Investigation*. New York: Teachers College Press, Columbia University.

Skolinspektionen. 2010. *Undervisning i Engelska i Grundskolan*. Skolinspektionen: (Sammanfattning), Rapport 2010:17 [Schools Inspectorate: Teaching English in Compulsory School. Summary, Report 2010:17].

Skolverket. 2004. *Engelska i Åtta Europeiska Länder – en Undersökning om Ungdomars Kunskaper och Uppfattningar*. Rapport 242. Stockholm: Fritzes Offentliga Publikationer [National Education Agency, English in Eight European Countries – A Survey of Teenagers' Knowledge and Opinions. Report 242].

Storch, N. 2001. "How Collaborative Is Pair Work? ESL Tertiary Students Composing in Pairs." *Language Teaching Research* 5 (1): 29–53.

Storch, N., and A. Aldosari. 2010. "Learners' Use of First Language (Arabic) in Pair Work in an EFL Class." *Language Teaching Research* 14 (4): 355–375.

Swain, M., and S. Lapkin. 2000. "Task-Based Second Language Learning: The Uses of the First Language." *Language Teaching Research* 4 (3): 251–274.

Toohey, K. 2000. *Learning English at School: Identity, Social Relations and Classroom Practice*. Clevedon: Multilingual Matters.

Van Lier, L. 2004. *The Ecology of Language Learning: A Sociocultural Perspective*. Boston, MA: Kluwer.

Vygotsky, L. S. 1978. *Mind in Society*. Cambridge, MA: Harvard University Press.

Warrington, M., and M. Younger. 2006. *Raising Boys' Achievement in Primary Schools: Towards a Holistic Approach*. Maidenhead: Open University Press.

Watanabe, Y., and M. Swain. 2007. "Effects of Proficiency Differences and Patterns of Pair Interaction on Second Language Learning: Collaborative Dialogue between Adult ESL Learners." *Language Teaching Research* 11 (2): 121–142.

Wells, G. 1999. *Dialogic Inquiry: Towards a Sociocultural Practice and Theory of Education*. Cambridge: Cambridge University Press.

Williams, M., and R. L. Burden. 1996. *Psychology for Language Teachers*. Oxford: Oxford University Press.

How to integrate cooperative skills training into learning tasks: an illustration with young pupils' writing

Katia Lehraus

Faculty of Psychology and Education Sciences, Section of Education Sciences, University of Geneva, Switzerland

> This study explored how to integrate cooperative skills training into learning tasks in the area of writing. Cooperative learning sessions, aimed at developing both cooperative and cognitive skills, were created and conducted in two elementary school classes (Grade 2, age 7–8). Pupils' teamwork interactions were videotaped and analysed. Results show that young pupils were able to work cooperatively on writing tasks (WT) without teacher's help, advocating realisable teaching practices. Interactive dynamics likely to enhance pupils' involvement in constructive interactions and in WT are documented; this typology could be used as a heuristic tool in future qualitative research.

Introduction

Many pedagogical approaches in most educational systems suggest fostering peer interaction in order to enhance learning. Peer learning (Topping 2005) includes various forms of acquiring knowledge and competence through active help among partners. While in peer tutoring (Baudrit 2002; King 1998) a more expert partner is guiding a less expert one in appropriation of knowledge and skills, interactions among status equals are expected within diverse forms of teamwork, such as collaborative or cooperative learning.

Collaborative learning is 'a coordinated, synchronous activity that is the result of a continued attempt to construct and maintain a shared conception of a problem' (Roschelle and Teasley 1995, 70), in situations where two or more individuals learn, or try to learn, together (Dillenbourg 1999). Cooperative learning is focused on how to design situations that engage students in such collaborative learning processes with their peers. Cooperative learning is a set of instructional methods in which students work together in small groups towards a group goal in a way that 'the success of one student helps other students to be successful' (Slavin 1987, 8). Teachers have to organise and structure the group work 'so as to promote the participation and learning of all group members in a cooperatively shared undertaking' (Davidson and Worsham 1992, xi–xii). Aimed at exploring how elementary school teachers can develop young pupils' interactions in learning tasks, this study is focused on equal status peer-mediated learning shaped by cooperative learning approaches.

In cooperative learning, peer interactions are structured by the teacher and based on a set of key principles defined by each method (for an overview of methods, see Sharan 1999). Cooperative learning methods and their beneficial effect on social and academic outcomes have been well documented for over 30 years (for meta-analyses, see Johnson et al. 1981; Roseth, Johnson, and Johnson 2008; Slavin 1983, 1996). Yet, a minor part of research concerns young pupils in elementary school. Can peer interaction benefit beginners in basic reading or writing as well as in development of basic social and cooperative skills? Research stresses the importance of preparing pupils to cooperate in order to enhance constructive interactions (Blatchford et al. 2006; Cohen 1994; Gillies 2003b; Johnson, Johnson, and Johnson Holubec 2002; Kutnick, Ota, and Berdondini 2008). However, social and cooperative skills training programmes are often separated from regular learning situations in classrooms and their outcomes are inconsistent (Ogilvy 2000).

The aim of this study is twofold: first, to explore how cooperative skills training can be integrated into teamwork learning tasks in elementary school, in the area of writing; second, to document peer interactions of young pupils engaged in such learning settings.

Theoretical background

Are young pupils really able to work in groups? This question is often raised by elementary school teachers. Extensive observations in early years of primary school in the UK (see the SPRinG project; Baines, Blatchford, and Webster 2015; Blatchford et al. 2006) indicate recurrent problems concerning teamwork functioning (Blatchford et al. 2003; Kutnick et al. 2008) and learning outcomes, unless students were prepared to work in groups (Baines, Blatchford, and Kutnick 2003). In addition, it is reported that teamwork is quite rarely used and that pupils are merely sitting in groups (Baines et al. 2003; Blatchford et al. 2003) instead of working together.

Cooperative learning

Cooperative learning is more than just sitting in groups. It is a set of instructional methods whereby pupils work in teams 'toward a common goal or outcome, or share a common problem or task in such a way that they can only succeed in completing the work through behaviour that demonstrates interdependence, while holding individual contributions and efforts accountable' (Brody and Davidson 1998, 8). Various approaches and methods exist, aimed at developing both academic achievement and social skills (Slavin 1996). 'Learning Together' (Johnson et al. 2002) was selected for this study as one of the most suitable methods for elementary school.

'Learning Together' is based on five key principles (Johnson et al. 2002). To follow them, a teacher has to: (1) assign pupils to teams in a way that group composition would foster helping interactions among members; (2) structure positive interdependence within teams in order to orient pupils' actions towards a common goal; (3) structure individual responsibility so that each member makes his or her contribution to the group task or goal; (4) develop pupils' cooperative skills to enhance social relations and constructive interactions among team members; and (5) organise group processing in order to improve group functioning.

The benefits of a cooperative learning method on pupils' achievement and social skills are dependent on its implementation: 'translating the promise of cooperative learning to practice is more complicated than meets the eye, and does not always guarantee that the desired goals of cooperative learning are achieved' (Sharan 2010, 301). In a survey where the majority (93%) of elementary school teachers reported regular use of cooperative learning, only very few (5%) met the 'Learning Together' five-element criterion (Antil et al. 1998). In another study, most of those elementary school teachers interviewed who claimed to use cooperative learning also admitted not having implemented explicit cooperative skills teaching in their classrooms (Lehraus 2002). An issue that should be developed more extensively in a teacher education perspective is how to put cooperative learning, and particularly cooperative skills, into practice.

Cooperative skills training

Teachers may often presume that pupils know how to work in groups. Conversely, teacher educators suggest that learning to cooperate is valuable when teachers expect pupils to cooperate for enhancing learning (Howden and Kopiec 2000; Rouiller and Howden 2010). A review of the literature on social skills training (Ogilvy 2000) shows that the evidence of effectiveness is mixed; social skills training may not be sufficient to improve an individual's social functioning. In schools, social skills training is often juxtaposed with learning tasks and the effects of such programmes are promising, but limited (Desbiens and Royer 2003). More investigation is needed on the role of pupil training for collaboration and its influence on learning outcomes (Prichard, Bizo, and Stratford 2006).

Some studies in elementary school show that social or cooperative skills training can enhance peer interaction and learning (Gillies 2000, 2003a; Jordan and Le Métais 1997; Kutnick et al. 2008). Positive effects were observed on cooperative behaviour, mutual help and exchange of information (Gillies and Ashman 1996, 1997, 1998), as well as on motivation towards teamwork, communication among partners and learning (Kutnick et al. 2008).

Taking time for cooperative skills training seems to be a key factor for positive effects on elementary school pupils' interactions and learning (Blatchford et al. 2006). Furthermore, in middle school, constructive peer interactions appear to be not only one of the positive effects of cooperative skills trainings but also one of the processes contributing to high-performance learning (Roseth et al. 2008). An issue worth exploring in elementary school is how cooperative skills training can develop constructive interactions among young pupils who are just beginners in fundamental skills such as learning to write.

Writing

Learning to write is a complex task, requiring simultaneous construction and mobilisation of processes that allow translation of ideas into a coherent text via handwriting (Olive et al. 2009). This complexity could be lessened by procedural facilitation (Bereiter and Scardamalia 1987) via external resources, such as checklists (Allal et al. 2001), or collaborative writing procedures (Roussey and Gombert 1992; Yarrow and Topping 2001).

The common practice of individual writing in classroom does not usually allow pupils to benefit from dialogue with peers (Yarrow and Topping 2001), nor from potential peer regulation (Allal et al. 2001) during interaction. Interactive situations could nevertheless increase cognitive load (Kirschner 2002), especially when young pupils become involved in cognitive and social processes at the same time. However, shared writing in a distributed cognition perspective (Salomon 2001) could lighten the intrinsic cognitive load (Verhoeven, Schnotz, and Paas 2009) of such a complex task for young pupils. A study with preschoolers (Morin and Montésinos-Gelet 2003) revealed that pupils' meta-linguistic comments during collaborative writing had an important impact on appropriation of writing and on the quality of output written in triads.

Collaborative writing (Baudrit 2007) takes various forms depending on text features and on writing phases concerned with collaboration (e.g. mutual revision and correction of individual texts, writing of a shared text consisting of individual parts, writing of a common text including collaborative planning, composition, revision and correction). Research on collaborative writing is mainly focused on processes; few studies are concerned with instructional design. In 'Paired Writing' (Yarrow and Topping 2001), authors suggest structuring collaborative writing by leaning on constructive mediators for learning, such as those described in peer tutoring: 'increased engagement and time spent on-task, immediacy and individualisation of help, goal specification, explaining, prevention of information-processing overload, prompting, modelling, reinforcement' (p. 262). Collaborative writing appears to be a broad area inviting teachers and researchers to create novel designs aimed at structuring pupils' interactions. Cooperative learning offers tools for such structures.

Cooperative learning with integrated cooperative skills training into writing tasks

For the purpose of this study, an instructional design based on the elements presented above was elaborated. While in 'Paired Writing' (Yarrow and Topping 2001) distinct roles (writer and helper) are assigned to partners in a tutoring scheme, this study's design leans on more symmetrical interactions; thus, it was structured with the five principles of 'Learning Together' (Johnson et al. 2002). In addition, an original cooperative skills training, suited for young pupils, was tailored for its incorporation into writing tasks (WT).

Research questions

This study was aimed at (A) elaborating and testing a classroom intervention which combines cooperative learning key principles, cooperative skills training and writing with elementary school pupils; (B) documenting pupils' interactions at the end of the intervention.

Analyses were oriented by three general questions: (1) How can pairs of young pupils engage in teamwork in writing? (2) Which interactive processes can be observed within paired interactions? (3) In which ways are social, cooperative and cognitive dimensions of interactive processes related?

Methodology

Classroom intervention

Two cooperative learning interventions were created, aimed at developing both cognitive and cooperative skills. The interventions were conducted in two classes (Grade 2, age 7–8) of an elementary school in Geneva (Switzerland), in November and March of the same school year. Each intervention was composed of eight tasks: four preparatory tasks (PT, five hours in sum) and four WT (eight hours in sum). Tasks were built on the basis of French language teaching material (Dolz, Noverraz, and Schneuwly 2001). Originally individual lessons were transformed into cooperative learning settings and structured with the key principles of 'Learning Together' (Johnson et al. 2002).

As space is lacking to present both interventions, which are similarly designed, only the second one (Figure 1) is described in this article. The aim of this second intervention was to

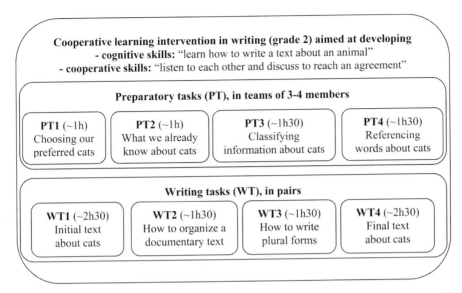

Figure 1. Second cooperative learning intervention in writing, integrating cooperative skills training.

'learn to write a text about an animal'. The cooperative skills training was focused on 'listen to each other and discuss, to reach an agreement'. In accordance with the textbook, a learning session in writing begins with an initial written production (WT1 in this study: pupil pairs had to write a first text about cats); it ends with a final written production, where the draft is improved (WT4 in this study: pupil pairs had to revise and correct their first text). These are certainly very complex tasks for beginners in writing; more specific learning tasks helped pupils to improve in-between (WT2 in this study: pupil pairs discovered how to organise a text; WT3: they exercised plural forms of nouns). There can be more than two specific tasks between the first and final text, depending on pupils' needs.

To lighten these obviously difficult WT and interlink them with 'listening to each other and discussing to reach an agreement', four original PT were created. These tasks introduced cooperative skills training and prepared pupils for the forthcoming WT. Cooperative skills training followed the 'Learning Together' principle of explicit social skills teaching, based on social learning (Bandura 1976, 2003). The weight of this principle of 'Learning Together' was increased: additional time and resources (checklists) were provided for cooperative skills teaching, and special attention was paid to design cooperative tasks where listening and discussing for agreement would be necessary to achieve writing.

To illustrate how cooperative skills and learning goals in writing were interconnected, PT3 and PT4 are presented (Figure 2). PT3 was aimed at 'listening to each other and discuss to reach an agreement' and 'classifying information about cats'. In a first whole-class phase, the teacher reminded pupils of the cooperative skill on the basis of a chart (Appendix 1); this chart was created in PT1 and enriched in PT2. Pupils had the opportunity to propose new ideas about 'what could be said or done' to improve use of this skill. For the second, interactive phase, pupils were assigned to groups of three or four members. Each group received a set of 20 different sheets of information about cats to be shared among members. Group members took turns to read one of the sheets in order to inform group mates, who had to listen carefully. Then, the group had to decide about the category (e.g. behaviour, food) for the sheet's classification. Again, group members had to listen to each other's

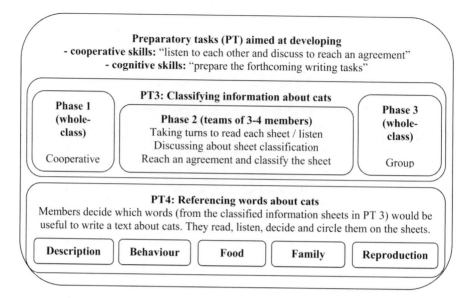

Figure 2. Illustration of two preparatory tasks (PT3 and PT4).

propositions and then reach an agreement to choose a category. In the third, whole-class phase, the teacher conducted group processing in reference to the cooperative skill chart.

A tool for writing (Appendix 2) was added to the tool for cooperation (Appendix 1). This chart for the forthcoming WT was constructed during the PT4. On the basis of the previous information classification (PT3), group members had to decide which words from the sheets would be useful as help for writing a text about cats. They had to listen to each other and reach an agreement to circle words chosen for the chart.

This illustration shows how both aims (cooperating and writing) are interwoven in PT and how meaningful tools were constructed to initiate and strengthen the development of cooperative skills as well as to support pupils' writing skills.

Sample and data collection

Four pupils in each class were selected by their teachers to be filmed ($N = 8$). The sample was gender-balanced (four boys and four girls) and French-level balanced (four high-level and four low-level pupils). Target pupils worked with different group mates according to the purpose of each task.

Interactions of four teams (including target pupils) in each class were videotaped throughout both interventions (16 tasks, 26 hours in sum). After a couple of sessions, pupils got used to the four cameras in the classroom and they did not seem to be aware of them anymore. Presented data concern interactions of eight teams (four in each class) in the last task of the second intervention (WT4): pupil pairs had to revise their first draft in order to write a final text about cats.

Data treatment and analyses

Three types of analyses were carried out to document pupils' interactions at the end of the whole-classroom intervention. First, observation was focused on pupil pairs' functioning

LEARNING TO LEARN TOGETHER

within teamwork to state how pairs engaged in assigned tasks. Secondly, in order to deepen understanding of this global functioning, investigation was centred on interactive processes within paired interactions and explored how social, cooperative and cognitive dimensions could shape pupils' interactive dynamics. Finally, to unravel the complexity of observed interactive dynamics, investigation focused on these three dimensions' relations within interactive processes and on their links with the evolution of the WT.

Global quantitative analysis

First-level analysis measured how much time each pair spent in different types of activity. Videotaped data were observed and coded with software Videograph (Rimmele 2002). Inspired by 'On-the-Spot [OTS] Observation Categories' (Blatchford et al. 2006), three coding variables were defined and adjusted to the data. This first-level analysis informs globally and quantitatively about the partner of interaction, the content of interaction and the pupils' participation in interaction.

In-depth qualitative analysis

For second-level analysis, videotaped data were transcribed in detail and subdivided into episodes ($N = 293$). Each episode was coded with a multidimensional coding system, elaborated for the purpose of this study on the basis of different frameworks whose categories were adjusted to the data. Three dimensions, closely linked together, were treated separately for analytical reasons: social, cooperative and cognitive dimensions of interactive processes.

Social dimension. Coding categories were inspired by an analytical framework for qualitative analysis (Kumpulainen and Mutanen 1999) and adjusted following methodological outlines used in studies aimed at investigating effects of cooperative learning and cooperative skills training on pupils' behaviour (Gillies 2000; Gillies and Ashman 1996, 1998). Four indicators for coding each episode were defined with reference to the trained cooperative skills: listening, dialogue, engagement and relational climate (e.g. gesture, tone of voice). Combination of codes across these four facets permitted rating of each episode as reflecting globally positive, negative or neutral social behaviour.

Cooperative dimension. Coding categories were built according to an analytical model intersecting three main lines: degree of symmetry, degree of agreement and degree of alignment (Baker 2002, 2008). Indicators were developed to code each episode in association with various forms of cooperation derived from Baker's model. By combining codes in these three main lines, each episode was rated as effective cooperation (when partners were aligned on the same object of interaction) or apparent cooperation (when not aligned).

Cognitive dimension. For this dimension, coding categories could not be elaborated following existing frameworks, which mostly examine the quality of language and the level of reasoning, such as 'disputational, cumulative or exploratory talk' (Mercer 1996). Indeed, data revealed rather poor verbalisations for such categories that seemed to better suit older pupils or other tasks. Three indicators for coding each episode were developed in a 'bottom-up' way: use of external resources, task treatment and task evolution in writing.

Statistical analysis

Third-level analysis was carried out on all episodes previously coded for the purpose of second-level qualitative in-depth analysis ($N = 293$). Inferential statistics inform relations

LEARNING TO LEARN TOGETHER

among social, cooperative and cognitive dimensions of interactive processes, as formerly disentangled.

Results and discussion

This classroom intervention study was carried out using key cooperative learning principles and integrating cooperative skills training into WT with Second Grade pupils (7–8 years old). Conducted in two elementary school classes, the study took place as planned. Pupils' interactions in the final part of the study, aimed at writing cooperatively a final text about cats, were recorded for examination.

In this article, only some results from the first (global) and third (statistical) analyses are presented, to give a general picture of this study's findings. Yet, the description of second (in-depth) analytical categories was required to allow understanding of how the data were treated in order to permit subsequent examination through statistical analysis.

All results concern paired teamwork, which means that analysed data include only the moments, but all the moments, where pupils were supposed to work together without teachers' help or supervision. Whole-class and teacher-led interventions are therefore not taken into account.

An insight into the global functioning of pupil pairs during teamwork

How did pupil pairs engage in teamwork writing? All pupil pairs were formed by the teacher, which means that each pupil had to work with a teammate he or she had not chosen. Considering the partner of interaction in paired teamwork (Table 1), the assigned peer appears to have been on average the partner with most interaction time (92.3% of all the time dedicated to paired teamwork), despite the fact that contrasted behaviours were also observed from one pair to another, notably for moments without partner (variation from 0% to 14.7%). Yet, young pupils were able to keep to the imposed structure and teammate without constant teacher supervision.

When looking at the content of interaction in paired teamwork (Table 2), most time (86.3% in average) concerned task-related matter. In these on-task interactions, sensibly more attention was paid to inherent task content than to task management. Off-task interactions were very limited in time (8.7% in average); the large variation (also visible during on-task time) is due to one specific pair in which one pupil displayed off-task behaviour in this precise setting. On the whole, pairs were rarely off-task, as might be feared with young pupils, notably if needing help or experiencing conflicts.

Finally, in terms of participation in paired interaction on-task with the assigned peer (Table 3), partners were mostly committed in interactive participation (84.7% in

Table 1. First-level analysis: partner of interaction in teamwork, for eight pairs in WT4 (percentage of total teamwork time).

Partner of interaction	WT4 (~46 minute)	
	Mean	Standard deviation
With assigned peer	92.3%	85.3–97.9
With another pupil	4.1%	0.0–9.8
Without partner (working alone)	3.6%	0.0–14.7

58

LEARNING TO LEARN TOGETHER

Table 2. First-level analysis: content of interaction in teamwork, for eight pairs in WT4 (percentage of total teamwork time).

	WT4 (~46 minute)	
Content of interaction	Mean	Standard deviation
On-task	86.3%	56.4–93.2
Task content	60.4%	41.7–76.5
Task management	25.9%	14.7–36.6
Off-task	8.7%	0.3–39.7
Other	5.0%	1.5–7.2

average). Pupils participated mainly in a joint manner (a common task or two interdependent tasks were completed together), then in a distributed way (one task was carried out by taking successive turns or two different tasks were completed separately at the same time). A minor amount of time was spent on individual participation (13.3%). These observations show that partners were able to contribute together and actively to assign WT.

Global analysis results are quite encouraging. Important interactive participation on-task with assigned partner indicates that the features of this classroom intervention seem to foster constructive behaviours for learning. These findings are consistent with promises of 'Learning Together' (Johnson et al. 2002), with research demonstrating globally positive effects of cooperative learning methods (Slavin 1996, 2015) and specifically with studies on social or cooperative skills trainings effects (Blatchford et al. 2006; Gillies 2000, 2003a, 2003b; Gillies and Ashman 1996, 1997, 1998; Kutnick et al. 2008).

A cooperative learning intervention with integrated cooperative skills training in writing tailored for elementary school thus appears to be a feasible practice, even with young pupils. Results show that a paired structure could be a factor of commitment in on-task interaction. This finding is consistent with the idea that extended on-task time could mediate constructive processes for learning (Yarrow and Topping 2001). Furthermore, it can be hypothesised that observed frequent interactive joint participation could foster these constructive processes through mutual help, exchange of explanations and cognitive load alleviation (Yarrow and Topping 2001). Such processes are not perceptible through this global analysis, but can be traced with in-depth investigation of interactive processes.

This kind of qualitative analysis was carried out (Lehraus 2010), but no enough space for its detailed presentation here. However, qualitative coding of episodes for this purpose permitted the unravelling of the complexity of interactive processes and deepened the understanding of ways in which social, cooperative and cognitive dimensions can shape pupils' interactive dynamics.

Table 3. First-level analysis: participation in interaction in teamwork, for eight pairs in WT4 (percentage of teamwork time on-task with assigned peer).

	WT4 (~33 minute)	
Participation in interaction	Mean	Standard deviation
Interactive participation	84.7%	76.7–95.3
Joint	70.1%	52.2–90.7
Distributed	14.6%	0.0–21.6
Individual	13.3%	3.6–21.3
Other	2.0%	0.3–5.9

LEARNING TO LEARN TOGETHER

Table 4.   Statistical analysis: crosstabs for social dimension (characteristics of social behaviour) and cooperative dimension (forms of cooperation), for eight pairs in WT4 (frequency, percentage per cell, percentage in line and in row).

Social behaviour	Cooperation						
	Effective		Apparent		Total	
Positive	134	45.7%	17	5.8%	151	51.5%
% in line		88.7%		11.3%		
% in row		65.0%		19.5%		
Neutral	50	17.1%	25	8.5%	75	25.6%
% in line		66.7%		33.3%		
% in row		24.3%		28.7%		
Negative	22	7.5%	45	15.4%	67	22.9%
% in line		32.8%		67.2%		
% in row		10.7%		51.7%		
Total	206	70.3%	87	29.7%	293	100%

Note: $X^2(2) = 70.12$, $p < .000$; Phi = .489.

An insight into interactive processes within functioning of pupil pairs in teamwork

How are social, cooperative and cognitive dimensions of interactive processes related? All episodes of on-task teamwork with assigned partner ($N = 293$), previously coded for these three dimensions, were examined. Social and cooperative dimensions, both concerned with cooperative skills training, were analysed together to consider how pairs interacted in the final setting of the classroom intervention (Table 4).

Three characteristics of social behaviour (positive, neutral and negative) were intersected with two forms of cooperation (effective and apparent). Margin totals of each dimension show an important percentage of social positive behaviour (51.5%) and of effective cooperation (70.3%). So the eight pairs spent half of on-task teamwork time in a positive atmosphere, characterised by listening, dialogue, engagement and good relational climate. Additionally, partners cooperated in an effective manner (aligned) during three quarters of episodes, which shows very frequent good quality communication.

Considering interrelations between social behaviour and forms of cooperation, a significant relation appears ($X^2(2) = 70.12$, $p < .000$); in addition, Phi coefficient (.489) shows a strong association between those dimensions. Looking at percentages in line, positive social behaviour is very frequently linked with effective cooperation (88.7%), but rarely with apparent cooperation (11.3%). Inversely, negative social behaviour is frequently associated with apparent cooperation (67.2%) and seldom with effective cooperation (32.8%). Results show that these two dimensions are statistically strongly related.

An exploratory typology of interactive dynamics

The findings presented above can be considered as an empirical indication for an exploratory typology of interactive dynamics (Table 5). In this perspective, episodes characterised by effective cooperation and positive social behaviour are called dynamics potentially favouring learning (FL), so as episodes characterised by apparent cooperation and negative social behaviour are called dynamics potentially not favouring learning (NFL). For the remaining episodes, in order to avoid overinterpretation of data, some are added to the NFL category and some are called neutral (N).

LEARNING TO LEARN TOGETHER

Table 5. Categories of interactive dynamics, proposed as a result from crossing social and cooperative dimensions of interactive processes.

	Cooperation	
Social behaviour	Effective	Apparent
Positive	FL	N
Neutral	N	NFL
Negative	NFL	NFL

Table 6. Distribution of episodes in exploratory typology of interactive dynamics crossed with evolution of the WT, for eight pairs in WT4 (frequency).

	Evolution of the WT			
Interactive dynamics	Positive	Neutral	Negative	Total
FL	106	26	2	134
Neutral for learning	38	25	4	67
NFL	45	31	16	92
Total	189	82	22	293

Three types of interactive dynamics (FL, neutral and NFL) were intersected with three modes of evolution of the WT (positive, neutral and negative). A significant relation appears ($X^2(4) = 33.84$, $p < .000$; Phi $= .340$), showing a clear link between these two dimensions (Appendix 3). The distribution of episodes ($N = 293$) in this exploratory typology (Table 6) illustrates that most episodes of interactive dynamics FL ended up in positive evolution of the WT (106). However, quite an important amount of not favouring dynamics (45) led to positive evolution in task as well. These episodes should be cautiously examined to gain more understanding.

Anchored in carefully analysed data, this exploratory typology is built on a solid empirical basis. Its main purpose is to be tested and refined with new sets of data from other elementary schools, and possibly serve as a heuristic tool for exploring interactive processes in further research.

Conclusion

Results can be summarised according to research questions. The elaborated classroom intervention, combining cooperative learning key principles, cooperative skills training and writing and tested in two Second Grade classes (age 7–8 years), turned out to be achievable with young pupils engaged in fundamental learning tasks. Data collected at the end of the whole intervention document the interactions of pupil pairs in the light of complementary analyses.

Generally, pairs were able to work cooperatively on WT without teacher help or supervision for a large amount of the time. Pupils displayed appropriate functioning by demonstrating huge commitment in on-task matter with the assigned partner in an interactive, mostly joint form of participation. These findings suggest that it seems possible to improve group work practice, often problematic with young pupils (Baines et al. 2003; Blatchford et al. 2003; Kutnick et al. 2008), on the strength of a cooperative learning structure and cooperative skills training; these features are close to the social pedagogy

LEARNING TO LEARN TOGETHER

approach of classroom group work developed in the SPRinG project (Baines et al. 2015; Blatchford et al. 2006).

Detailed examination of interactive processes during pupil interactions revealed that social and cooperative dimensions were statistically strongly related: positive social behaviour and effective cooperation were very frequently associated. An exploratory typology defined these promising interactive dynamics as likely to enhance pupils' involvement in constructive interactions for learning; they led quite often to positive development of the WT. These findings can be linked with constructive mediators for learning, notably immediacy of mutual help and prevention of information-processing overload (Yarrow and Topping 2001).

All these results are encouraging, but also limited, in relation to pupils' age. In the early years of elementary school, pupils may not have the necessary cognitive and social prerequisites to engage in elaborate interactions and reasoning. Relatively poor level of discussion is therefore not surprising and fits similar findings (Kershner et al. 2014) showing how social interaction can add complexity to learning tasks. Yet, this study provides empirical findings concerning young pupils, which are underrepresented in the literature on cooperative learning.

Progress in quality of interaction is probably associated with pupils' age, but also with their experience in cooperative learning. As teacher educators suggest (Howden and Kopiec 2000; Rouiller and Howden 2010; Sharan 2010), learning to cooperate is necessary to be able to cooperate to learn. This suggestion is illustrated by a study conducted in the final years of primary school, linking quality of pupil conversation to stages of development of collaboration (Kumpulainen and Kaartinen 2000). Pupils' experience of cooperation is also shaped by quality of implementation of cooperative learning in classrooms (Sharan 2010).

The issue of implementation of cooperative learning opens perspectives on teacher education. Should teacher professional development include experiential learning among teachers, acting as co-operators during teacher training sessions (Cohen, Brody, and Sapon-Shevin 2004), in school projects (Kasikova and Dubec 2009) or through collaboration between schools (Jolliffe and Hutchinson 2007)? There are surely new paths to follow (see Jolliffe, 2015) to create promising conditions for pupils' cooperation in classrooms.

References

Allal, L., D. Bétrix Köhler, L. Rieben, Y. Rouiller Barbey, M. Saada-Robert, and E. Wegmuller. 2001. *Apprendre l'orthographe en produisant des textes*. Fribourg: Editions Universitaires Fribourg Suisse.

Antil, L. R., R. J. Jenkins, K. S. Wayne, and F. P. Vadasy. 1998. "Cooperative Learning: Prevalence, Conceptualisations, and the Relation Between Research and Practice." *American Educational Research Journal* 35 (3): 419–454.

Baines, E., P. Blatchford, and P. Kutnick. 2003. "Changes in Grouping Practices Over Primary and Secondary School." *International Journal of Educational Research* 39 (1–2): 9–34.

Baines, E., P. Blatchford, and R. Webster. 2015. "The Challenges of Implementing Group-work in Primary School Classrooms and Including Pupils with special educational needs." *Education 3–13* 43 (1): 15–29.

Baker, J. M. 2002. "Forms of Cooperation in Dyadic Problem-Solving." *Revue d'Intelligence Artificielle* 16 (4–5): 587–620.

Baker, J. M. 2008. "Formes et processus de la résolution coopérative de problèmes: des savoirs aux pratiques éducatives." In *Vers des apprentissages en coopération: rencontres et perspectives*, edited by Y. Rouiller and K. Lehraus, 112–135. Berne: Peter Lang – Exploration.

LEARNING TO LEARN TOGETHER

Bandura, A. 1976. *L'apprentissage Social*. Translated by J. Rondal. Liège: Mardaga.

Bandura, A. 2003. *Auto-efficacité: le sentiment d'efficacité personnelle*. Bruxelles: De Boeck.

Baudrit, A. 2002. *Le tutorat: richesses d'une méthode pédagogique*. Bruxelles: De Boeck.

Baudrit, A. 2007. *L'apprentissage collaboratif: plus qu'une méthode collective?* Bruxelles: De Boeck.

Bereiter, C., and M. Scardamalia. 1987. *Fostering Self-Regulation. The Psychology of Written Composition*, 249–277. Hillsdale, NJ: Lawrence Erlbaum.

Blatchford, P., E. Baines, C. Rubie-Davies, P. Basset, and A. Chowne. 2006. "The Effect of a New Approach to Group Work on Pupil–Pupil and Teacher–Pupil Interactions." *Journal of Educational Psychology* 98 (4): 750–765.

Blatchford, P., P. Kutnick, E. Baines, and M. Galton. 2003. "Toward a Social Pedagogy of Classroom Group Work." *International Journal of Educational Research* 39 (1–2): 153–172.

Brody, C. M., and N. Davidson. 1998. *Professional Development for Cooperative Learning: Issues and Approaches*. Albany: State University of New York.

Cohen, E. G. 1994. "Restructuring the Classroom: Conditions for Productive Small Groups." *Review of Educational Research* 64 (1): 1–35.

Cohen, E. G., C. Brody, and M. Sapon-Shevin, eds. 2004. *Teaching Cooperative Learning: The Challenge for Teacher Education*. Albany, NY: Suny Press.

Davidson, N., and T. Worsham. 1992. *Enhancing Thinking Through Cooperative Learning*. New York: Teachers College Press.

Desbiens, N., and E. Royer. 2003. "Peer Groups and Behaviour Problems: A Study of School-Based Intervention for Children with EBD." *Emotional and Behavioural Difficulties* 8 (2): 120–139.

Dillenbourg, P. 1999. "What Do You Mean by 'Collaborative Learning'?" In *Collaborative Learning: Cognitive and Computational Approaches*, edited by P. Dillenbourg, 1–19. Oxford: Elsevier Science.

Dolz, J., M. Noverraz, and B. Schneuwly, eds. 2001. *S'exprimer en français: séquences didactiques pour l'oral et l'écrit* (Vol. I: 1ère/2ème. Notes méthodologiques avec CD-ROM et documents reproductibles). Bruxelles: De Boeck.

Gillies, R. M. 2000. "The Maintenance of Cooperative and Helping Behaviours in Cooperative Groups." *British Journal of Educational Psychology* 70 (1): 97–111.

Gillies, R. M. 2003a. "Structuring Co-operative Learning Experiences in Primary School." In *Co-operative Learning: The Social and Intellectual Outcomes of Learning in Groups*, edited by R. M. Gillies and A. F. Ashman, 36–53. London: Routledge Falmer.

Gillies, R. M. 2003b. "Structuring Cooperative Group Work in Classrooms." *International Journal of Educational Research* 39 (1–2): 35–49.

Gillies, R. M., and F. A. Ashman. 1996. "Teaching Collaborative Skills to Primary School Children in Classroom-Based Work Groups." *Learning and Instruction* 6 (3): 187–200.

Gillies, R. M., and F. A. Ashman. 1997. "The Effects of Training in Cooperative Learning on Differential Student Behavior and Achievement." *Journal of Classroom Interaction* 32 (1): 1–10.

Gillies, R. M., and F. A. Ashman. 1998. "Behavior and Interactions of Children in Cooperative Groups in Lower and Middle Elementary Grades." *Journal of Educational Psychology* 90 (4): 746–757.

Howden, J., and M. Kopiec. 2000. *Ajouter aux compétences: enseigner, coopérer et apprendre au postsecondaire*. Montréal: La Chenelière/McGraw-Hill.

Johnson, D. W., T. R. Johnson, and E. Johnson Holubec. 2002. *Circles of Learning: Cooperation in the Classroom*. 5th ed. Edina, MN: Interaction Book Company.

Johnson, D. W., G. Maruyama, T. R. Johnson, D. Nelson, and L. Skon. 1981. "Effects of Cooperative, Competitive, and Individualistic Goal Structures on Achievement: A Meta-Analysis. [Meta-Analysis]." *Psychological Bulletin* 89 (1): 47–62.

Jolliffe, W. 2015. "Bridging the Gap: Teachers Cooperating Together to Implement Cooperative Learning." *Education 3–13* 43 (1): 70–82.

Jolliffe, W., and H. Hutchinson. 2007. "Implementing Cooperative Learning in a Networked Learning Community." *Education 3–13: International Journal of Primary, Elementary and Early Years Education* 35 (1): 5–16.

Jordan, D. W., and J. Le Métais. 1997. "Social Skilling Through Cooperative Learning." *Educational Research* 39 (1): 3–21.

Kasikova, H., and M. Dubec. 2009. "Spoluprace ucitelu: od vetsi k mensi nezname." *Studia Paedagogica* 14 (1): 67–86.

LEARNING TO LEARN TOGETHER

Kershner, R., P. Warwick, N. Mercer, and J. Kleine Staarman. 2014. "Primary Children's Management of Themselves and Others in Collaborative Groupwork: 'Sometimes it takes Patience … '." *Education 3–13* 42 (2): 201–216.

King, A. 1998. "Transactive Peer Tutoring: Distributing Cognition and Metacognition." *Educational Psychology Review* 10 (1): 57–74.

Kirschner, P. A. 2002. "Cognitive Load Theory: Implications of Cognitive Load Theory on the Design of Learning. [Guest Editorial]." *Learning and Instruction* 12 (1): 1–10.

Kumpulainen, K., and S. Kaartinen. 2000. "Situational Mechanisms of Peer Group Interaction in Collaborative Meaning-Making: Processes and Conditions for Learning." *European Journal of Psychology of Education* 15 (4): 431–454.

Kumpulainen, K., and M. Mutanen. 1999. "The Situated Dynamics of Peer Group Interaction: An Introduction to an Analytic Framework." *Learning and Instruction* 9 (5): 449–473.

Kutnick, P., C. Ota, and L. Berdondini. 2008. "Improving the Effects of Group Working in Classrooms with Young School-Aged Children: Facilitating Attainment, Interaction and Classroom Activity." *Learning and Instruction* 18 (1): 83–95.

Lehraus, K. 2002. "La pédagogie coopérative: de la formation à la mise en pratique." *Revue suisse des sciences de l'éducation* 24 (3): 517–538.

Lehraus, K. 2010. "Développer les interactions entre élèves en situation d'apprentissage coopératif." Doctoral diss., University of Geneva.

Mercer, N. 1996. "The Quality of Talk in Children's Collaborative Activity in the Classroom." *Learning and Instruction* 6 (4): 359–377.

Morin, M.-F., and I. Montésinos-Gelet. 2003. "Les commentaires métagraphiques en situation collaborative d'écriture chez des enfants de maternelle." *Archives de Psychologie* 70 (272–73): 41–65.

Ogilvy, C. M. 2000. "Social Skills Training with Children and Adolescents: A Review of the Evidence on Effectiveness." In *Psychology of Education: Major Themes* (Vol. IV, Social Behaviour and the School Peer Group), edited by P. K. Smith and A. D. Pellegrini, 242–254. London: Routledge/Falmer.

Olive, T., M. Favart, C. Beauvais, and L. Beauvais. 2009. "Children's Cognitive Effort and Fluency in Writing: Effects of Genre and of Handwriting Automatisation." *Learning and Instruction* 19 (4): 299–308.

Prichard, J. S., L. A. Bizo, and J. R. Stratford. 2006. "The Educational Impact of Team-Skills Training: Preparing Students to Work in Groups." *British Journal of Educational Psychology* 76 (1): 119–140.

Rimmele, R. 2002. *Videograph. Multimedia Player zur Kodierung von Videos*. Kiel: IPN.

Roschelle, J., and D. S. Teasley. 1995. "The Construction of Shared Knowledge in Collaborative Problem Solving." In *Computer-Supported Collaborative Learning*, edited by C. E. O'Malley, 69–197. Berlin: Springer.

Roseth, C. J., W. D. Johnson, and T. R. Johnson. 2008. "Promoting Early Adolescents' Achievement and Peer Relationships: The Effects of Cooperative, Competitive, and Individualistic Goal Structures." *Psychological Bulletin* 134 (2): 223–246.

Rouiller, Y., and J. Howden. 2010. *La pédagogie coopérative: reflets de pratiques et approfondissements*. Montréal: Chenelière.

Roussey, J.-Y., and A. Gombert. 1992. "Ecriture en dyade d'un texte argumentatif par des enfants de huit ans." *Archives de Psychologie* 60 (235): 279–315.

Salomon, G. 2001. "No Distribution Without Individuals' Cognition: A Dynamic Interactional View." In *Distributed Cognitions: Psychological and Educational Considerations*, edited by G. Salomon, 111–138. Cambridge: Cambridge University Press.

Sharan, S., ed. 1999. *Handbook of Cooperative Learning Methods*. Westport, CT: Greenwood Press.

Sharan, Y. 2010. "Cooperative Learning for Academic and Social Gains: Valued Pedagogy, Problematic Practice." *European Journal of Education* 45 (2): 300–313.

Slavin, R. E. 1983. "When Does Cooperative Learning Increase Student Achievement?" *Psychological Bulletin* 94 (3): 429–445.

Slavin, R. E. 1987. *Cooperative Learning: Student Teams*. Washington, DC: National Education Association.

Slavin, R. E. 1996. "Research on Cooperative Learning and Achievement: What We Know, What We Need to Know." *Contemporary Educational Psychology* 21 (1): 43–69.

Slavin, R. E. 2015. "Cooperative Learning in Elementary Schools." *Education 3–13* 43 (1): 5–14.

Topping, K. J. 2005. "Trends in Peer Learning." *Educational Psychology* 25 (6): 631–645.

LEARNING TO LEARN TOGETHER

Verhoeven, L., W. Schnotz, and F. Paas. 2009. "Cognitive Load in Interactive Knowledge Construction." *Learning and Instruction* 19 (5): 369–375.

Yarrow, F., and J. K. Topping. 2001. "Collaborative Writing: The Effects of Metacognitive Prompting and Structured Peer Interaction." *British Journal of Educational Psychology* 71 (2): 261–282.

Appendix 1. Co-constructed chart for cooperation

Listen to each other and discuss to reach an agreement	
What we can do	What we can say
• Look at the one who is speaking • Ask before speaking • Move the head to show agreement or disagreement • Suggest an idea and ask others if they agree or not • ...	• 'Please' • 'Don't cut me short when I'm speaking' • 'Let's both of us give an idea' • 'I don't agree with your idea' • 'Do you agree with me?' • 'Can you tell me why you disagree with me?' • ...

Appendix 2. Co-constructed chart for writing

Behaviour of cats		
Nouns	Verbs	Other words
Balance	To climb	Nimble
Basket	To meow	Slowly
...	...	...

Note: Similar charts were elaborated for other useful categories to write a text (e.g. food, description, reproduction, etc.).

Appendix 3. Statistical analysis: crosstabs for interactive dynamics and evolution of the WT, for eight pairs in WT4 (frequency, percentage per cell, percentage in line and in row)

Interactive dynamics	Evolution of the WT							
	Positive		Neutral		Negative		Total	
FL	106	36.2%	26	8.9%	2	0.7%	134	45.7%
% in line		79.1%		19.4%		1.5%		
% in row		56.1%		31.7%		9.1%		
Neutral for learning	38	13.0%	25	8.5%	4	1.4%	67	22.9%
% in line		56.7%		37.3%		6.0%		
% in row		20.1%		30.5%		18.2%		
NFL	45	15.4%	31	10.6%	16	5.5%	92	31.4%
% in line		48.9%		33.7%		17.4%		
% in row		23.8%		37.8%		72.7%		
Total	189	64.5%	82	28.0%	22	7.5%	293	100%

Note: $X^2(4) = 33.84$, $p < .000$; Phi $= .340$.

Bridging the gap: teachers cooperating together to implement cooperative learning

Wendy Jolliffe

Faculty of Education, University of Hull, UK

> Cooperative learning (CL), in spite of extensive research and documented benefits, is not widely used in England. A review of the literature shows that it requires a staged and sustained approach to implementation, which has led to a gap between its potential and actual use. The case study cited here provides one example of bridging that gap through schools working together, with a community of facilitators, or experts, to provide support. As interest grows internationally into teachers cooperating in professional learning communities, this article argues that collaborative cultures provide the key to implementing and sustaining CL. In other words: teachers cooperating together also support pupils learning together.

Introduction

Cooperation and teamwork are widely advocated, crossing disciplinary boundaries from business to social sciences and education. According to Decuyper et al. (2010, 112), this has created a: 'babel like confusion' over what such concepts involve. Terms such as collaborative group work, peer learning, teamwork and cooperative learning (CL) are often used interchangeably when referring to education. Academics and practitioners who have spent considerable time researching and working in the field have identified crucial aspects that help define CL. According to Johnson and Johnson (2000), Slavin (1995), Kagan (1994), Cohen (1994), Sharan and Sharan (1992, 1994), these are: *positive interdependence*, where group members perceive that they are linked with each other and one member cannot succeed unless everyone does. Linked to this is the necessity for *individual accountability* to exist, where each member of the group must be accountable for his or her share of the work. Other factors include time for *group and individual reflection* where groups monitor and assess their functioning and ensure the development of the necessary *social and small group skills* for groups to function successfully. Based on the foregoing, the definition of CL used here is: *pupils working together in small groups on a joint task which ensures positive interdependence and individual accountability, underpinned by the pre-requisite small group and social skills.*

Research over four decades has demonstrated the benefits of CL as both supporting academic achievement and developing interpersonal skills (Jenkins et al. 2003; Johnson and Johnson 1975, 1989; Sharan 1990; Slavin 1995, 1996). This has led to the growth in the use of CL around the world and an International Association for the Study of Cooperation in Education, established in 1979. As much of the research is dated nearly 20 years ago, a more recent meta-analysis (Kyndt et al. 2013) set out to examine if the earlier claims were still valid and concluded that

> After taking a look at 11 review studies and Hattie's (2009) synthesis of the meta-analyses on this subject, it can be concluded that cooperation has relatively consistent positive effects on achievement, attitudes and other variables. (Kyndt et al. 2013, 137)

In the UK, the use of CL has been limited. Indeed, the practice of pupils working together cooperatively to support each other's learning is a relatively rare phenomenon (Baines, Blatchford, and Kutnick 2003; Kutnick et al. 2007) and is described as a 'neglected art' (Galton and Hargreaves 2009, 1). In order to address this, one study into group work in the UK, *the Social Pedagogic Research into Grouping* (SPRinG) (Blatchford et al. 2003, 2005), examined the potential of group work to influence learning, motivation, relationships and pupils' attitudes to learning, and a year-long intervention project to improve the use of group work in schools. Baines et al. (2015) provide further details of this project.

The SPRinG project focused on four important dimensions which facilitate effective group work: the physical organisation of the classroom; the development of pupils' group working skills; the structuring of tasks that legitimise group work and the supportive involvement of teachers and other adults during the group work. All of these factors resonate with other research in the area (Gillies and Boyle 2010; Johnson and Johnson 1998; Sharan 1990; Slavin 1995), but this article argues the development of collaborative cultures in schools, to sustain such ways of working, is the key to long-term success.

A number of research studies have explored factors in implementing CL. The next section examines these before going on to compare them with the findings from one case study that demonstrated success.

Implementation of CL

Research into the implementation of CL (Brody and Davidson 1998; Gillies 2003; Johnson and Johnson 1996; Stevahn et al. 2000) indicates that there are three main phases in this process: first, pre-training preparation, such as examining theoretical perspectives and reconciling personal beliefs about learning; second, the training itself, which is best undertaken through experiencing CL, and finally, post-training support to ensure long-term success. These phases can be further broken down into steps.

Understand the theoretical basis

Studies show that understanding the underlying theoretical basis for CL together with a research-validated rationale is an important precursor to implementation (Brody and Davidson 1998; Johnson and Johnson 1998; Sharan 2010). CL has evolved from a number of theoretical and psychological perspectives about learning. Slavin (2015) summarises the main roots of CL and integrates these into a model that he argues helps explain how CL impacts on learning. The perspective that is viewed by many researchers as fundamental to explaining the effectiveness of this way of learning is termed 'social interdependence'

(Deutsch 1949; Johnson, Johnson, and Holubec 1998; Schmuck and Schmuck 2001). This theory is derived from the work of Dewey (1916), and Lewin (1948), and later developed by Deutsch (1949) into a theory of social interdependence, which explains that each member of a group will cooperate for a goal when each understands that everyone's efforts contribute to the group's success.

Reconcile existing beliefs

It is important to not only examine the underlying research-validated theoretical perspectives, as previously mentioned, but also to relate these to a teacher's personal conceptions about effective learning. Brody's research into professional development for teachers in CL (Brody 1998) highlighted that a failure to connect the values implicit in an innovation with the teacher's own beliefs can result in problems in adopting new methods. In particular, teachers' beliefs regarding the locus of control and authority in teaching, the nature of knowledge and the teacher's role in decision-making are significant. Brody cites a framework (1992) to examine general epistemological assumptions, which she finds assists in 'breaking down stereotypes and assumptions about colleagues, and facilitating reflective professional development practices' (Brody 1998, 28).

Experience CL first-hand

Studies also identify the value of teachers experiencing cooperative group work first-hand in any training they undertake (Johnson and Johnson 1998; Rolheiser and Stevahn 1998; Roy 1998). As Brody (2004, 187) comments: 'Experiencing cooperative learning is at the core of being able to understand it and eventually transfer and apply its principles to classrooms.' Training should also help teachers to make conscious connections between this approach and their own classrooms and understand how to adapt CL to their contexts (Baines, Blatchford, and Kutnick 2003; Gillies 2008).

Gradually build confidence

Equally important is the need to consider teachers' feelings of self-worth or self-efficacy. As Cooper and Boyd (1998) acknowledge this is important for children's learning, but even more so with adults. For teachers a new approach needs testing over time, gradually moulding it to an individual teacher's style. In this way a teacher gains confidence and competence. In effect this means that teachers should have opportunities to try out new approaches using a self-directed learning process whilst ensuring continuous guided reflection and discussion. It is through working with peers that such reflection can be deepened to help further improvements in practice.

Collaborate and co-coach

Rolheiser and Stevahn (1998) emphasise the importance of working in collaborative school cultures that support continuous learning. Long-term success requires the creation of collegial teams or small cooperative groups (from two to five members) whose purpose is to work together to continually improve each other's success in using CL (Johnson and Johnson 1994). This requires coaching in teams using such activities as co-teaching cooperative lessons providing feedback and encouragement (Johnson and Johnson 1998; Schmuck 1998).

Sustain in learning communities

Implementing CL requires a sustained and collaborative process to be effective (Johnson and Johnson 1998). In other words: it is not a 'quick fix' as 'changing instructional practices takes decades not days' (Johnson and Johnson 1998, 224). This is a far cry from what was once seen as common practice for teachers: the one-day training course, which was delivered in a 'top-down' fashion, with little evidence of transfer to the classroom (Bottery and Wright 2000). Examination of research findings into different forms of professional development (Kennedy 2005) shows they range from 'transmissive' at one end (illustrated by the one-day training course) to 'transformative' at the other end. The 'transformative' model consists of a fusion of co-coaching and action research within communities of practice. Such communities are teacher-centred, context-specific and view professional development as being owned by the participants. This has its roots in a social theory of learning, or 'communities of practice' (Lave and Wenger 1991). This paper argues that in order to implement CL in the classroom, teachers themselves need to work cooperatively with colleagues in a learning community.

In the USA, England and particularly Singapore, there is a growing interest in teachers working together, developing professional learning communities (PLCs), as a vehicle for professional development. No common definition of PLCs exists although there is a consensus that it involves groups of teachers who come together to interrogate their practice in an on-going reflective collaborative way and engage in continuous cycles of inquiry-based teacher learning (DuFour et al. 2010; Hargreaves and Fullan 2012; Hord 1997; McLauglin and Talbert 2006). Governments have showed particular interest in developing PLCs because as Stoll et al. (2006, 221) state they 'hold considerable promise for capacity building for sustainable improvement'. Although evidence of the impact of PLCs has been provided in several large-scale studies (Bolam et al. 2005; Harris and Jones 2011), Feger and Arruda (2008) note, they 'are generally more descriptive than rigorous in [their] methods' (2008, 12). There is therefore a need to provide more evidence into how such communities can be developed and sustained.

In England, the concept of teachers working together undertaking 'joint practice development' is being promoted by the National College for School Leadership (NCSL 2012). This is defined as 'a process by which individuals, schools or other organisations learn from one another' (NCSL 2012, 7). Bold claims are made for this form of professional development, but with limited evidence to date of how it should be developed, or its impact, other than a report commissioned by the NCSL (Sebba, Kent, and Tregenza 2010),

There is a growing momentum internationally for teachers to work together to support professional development. As the foregoing review of research into implementing CL shows, this needs to be a staged and a sustained collaborative process. In a climate of rapid reform and accountability in England and elsewhere, this presents considerable challenges for schools due to the long-term nature of such an implementation process.

In spite of such challenges, success in implementing CL was documented in one network of schools in England. The next section will examine this network in order to ascertain how this was achieved and whether any of the factors from the foregoing review into implementation contributed to its success.

Case study

Research context

The research was carried out in a networked learning community (NLC) in an area of high social and economic deprivation in the North of England, over five years between 2004 and

LEARNING TO LEARN TOGETHER

2009. The network consisted of 2 secondary schools and 10 primary schools, although 2 schools were later closed due to falling pupil numbers. The NLCs government-funded initiative introduced in 1999 contained many elements of Wenger's concept of 'communities of practice' (1998), including mutual engagement, joint understanding and developing a joint repertoire of skills. It focused on networks of schools as well as creating learning communities within schools and shares many similarities with PLCs, but differed in having a focus on networks *of* schools rather than networks *within* schools. NLCs grew from 1999, aided by the support of the NCSL, because as Lieberman (1999, 2) states:

> they encourage and seem to support many of the key ideas that reformers say are needed to produce change and improvement in schools, teaching, and learning.

The NCSL made bold claims for NLCs' programme, stating that it became the largest programme of its kind in the world. More than 134 school networks took part, involving approximately 35,000 staff and over 675,000 pupils. The programme was fully launched in 2001 by NCSL and ran until 2006, culminating in 137 networks, though many networks continued to develop after that date and went on to evolve into other forms of partnership. The demise of funding for the project was largely attributed to a lack of evidence of impact and the way in which networks work (Katz and Earl 2010). In spite of this, the NCSL's website claimed that 'through their work, these groups of schools demonstrated the massive potential benefits that can come from working together' (NCSL 2007). Research into networks (Cordingley et al. 2006; Earl et al. 2006; Lieberman 1999) identified certain important ingredients for success: a shared purpose and focus; collaboration of all parties; the commitment of head teachers; a mixture of information sharing and psychological support and an effective facilitator.

The schools in the NLC that formed the context for this research had a long history of working together and previously they had been part of an Education Action Zone (EAZ), a government initiative with the aim of raising standards and providing additional support in areas of deprivation. Even after the funding ceased for NLCs, this network continued to thrive and the research identified a key factor as the strong relationships that existed, particularly between headteachers (Jolliffe 2011). The shared focus for the network was to impact on pupils' learning through the use of CL. By 2008, initial research indicated that over a period of five years, the central aim of implementing CL had been achieved. Questionnaires completed by teachers in 10 schools indicated a 100% ($n = 97$) response to the use of CL in classrooms, which included both informal paired work as well as more formal established groups working together, which is considered more difficult to implement. Teachers' responses regarding their confidence in using CL showed a total of 85.7% of respondents reported that they were either confident or very confident in using CL and over 90% of teachers saw a positive impact on pupils from the use of CL (for further details, see Jolliffe 2011; Jolliffe and Hutchinson 2007). How this was achieved became the subject of further research.

Aims

The aims of the research then were to both verify the successful implementation of CL and to examine how it was achieved, through gathering a detailed picture of this learning community in the form of a case study. As Bassey states: 'Case study is study of a singularity conducted in depth in natural settings' (1999, 47). Whilst generalisations are problematic from such single cases and Bassey describes them as 'fuzzy' (1999, 44), Yin's (2009, 39) concept of 'analytic generalisations' is helpful as it recommends using previously generated theory and research as a template to compare with empirical results from a case study. This process will be used here to propose generalisations that may have wider applicability.

The study aimed to provide a detailed picture of this NLC and examined what was the impact of the network in implementing CL. The methodology for this study consisted of gathering the views of stakeholders, including: headteachers, the CL facilitators (coordinators) and focus groups of pupils from each school to ascertain what had supported the implementation of CL. Semi-structured interviews were carried out with each headteacher and facilitator, together with observations in seven of the schools followed by focus group interviews with pupils from the lessons observed. Documentary analysis of termly minutes of meetings of the facilitators group over five years provided an additional source of data on the implementation of CL. This provided triangulation of methods to support the findings.

Results

The study examined three specific aspects:

(1) Key features of this network of schools
(2) The extent of the use of CL
(3) The methods of implementation used

Each of these will be discussed in turn before reflecting on their combined impact.

The nature of the network

The nature of the network was explored through interviews with headteachers and facilitators in 2008. This highlighted partnership and mutual support, and clearly indicated that the role of the network provided independence and ownership over the curriculum. Such independence had led the network, in its earlier form as an EAZ in 2000, to adopt a very different method of teaching literacy: *Success for All*, which is based on Slavin's model of CL (1996) and originated from the USA, to support all pupils to acquire essential literacy skills.

The introduction of the *Success for All* literacy programme in four primary schools in the network in 2000 provided the stimulus to develop the underpinning pedagogy used in this programme of CL, across all schools in the network in 2003. The repeated mention of the network supporting 'innovation' and developments in pedagogy by headteachers and some facilitators from interviews showed that the network 'was ahead of the game' (Headteacher 10), in innovating teaching approaches. This was largely due to the level of independence the network afforded the schools, so that they were 'totally independent from the Local Authority' as one long-standing headteacher acknowledged. This was because of a group of 'risk-taking heads' who were able to make 'the judgements and the decisions' (Headteacher 10). Without such a level of independence, implementing a totally different pedagogy in a climate of heavy prescription of the curriculum and teaching methods at that time, such as the National Literacy and Numeracy Strategy, would have been extremely difficult. In other words, the network provided the support to be innovative.

The fact that the network could do this was largely dependent on the nature of the network, and analysis of the interviews with headteachers and facilitators showed that the strength of the network revolved around the relationships that had been built, based on mutual trust and support and a sense of altruism.

LEARNING TO LEARN TOGETHER

we were all learning together and I think we can learn from each other, when one school has got one strength we can pawn that and I think it gels us all together more (Headteacher 9)

... an incredible camaraderie really so anybody will do anything for anybody else (Headteacher 5)

The analysis of these interviews showed the frequency of the following words: *trust, partnership, honesty*, and *support*.

Such partnership had been built up over time, with a number of headteachers knowing each other and working together for many years, as Headteacher 10 commented:

I think it was to do with relationships. One of the huge advantages was that we had a group of headteachers who had known each other for 20/30 years.

Nevertheless, there were considerable changes in personnel from 2003 to 2009 and the network continued to the extent that one headteacher talked of its evolution to a 'soft federation' (Headteacher 6). Relationships were important, but another factor that contributed to this network was the role of key personnel. Over half of headteachers interviewed mentioned this, and as Headteacher 11 stated: 'you need people to do that facilitating role'.

The facilitators' group that developed from 2005 until 2009 as a PLC within the network proved powerful in the cross-fertilisation of practices, resources and a source of psychological support. The agenda for the group was driven by the needs of the schools and provided a wealth of resources, including a handbook for staff, support for in-house training and visits to each other's schools to observe good practice. This expertise was in turn was cascaded by the facilitator to staff in schools. Interviews with facilitators highlighted the value placed on the facilitators' meetings and focused on two aspects: *sharing and support*, i.e. sharing information and resources and supporting each other in implementation. Comments included:

You can discuss pitfalls and problems and things that people found useful (Facilitator 1)
The meetings are really useful because we can share ideas (Facilitator 5)
It does help because especially when we've had the sharing opportunities which shared ideas for staff meetings ... we've shared resources and how they've been useful ... we've had ideas about what it looks like in other schools. (Facilitator 7)

In one case, specific mention was made of the relationships established through the network and the level of honesty and trust that enabled such sharing and support, for example:

You've got the support of your colleagues and are working together. (Facilitator 3)

The impact of the network in supporting innovation, in terms of pedagogy, was also commented on, for example:

I think it's been useful in terms of self-development hasn't it? It's developed the leader in order to better be able to develop others. (Facilitator 7)

In addition to the interviews, facilitators completed an annual questionnaire that reviewed progress. The comments of facilitators in December 2007 showed the value they placed on this PLC, for example:

LEARNING TO LEARN TOGETHER

> The opportunity to work alongside likeminded colleagues has been invaluable. It has been great to develop my own knowledge of not only cooperative learning but also thinking skills and then cascade this to other members of staff. (Respondent 3)

> I have been able to work alongside colleagues from other schools and develop resources cooperatively. We have developed our expertise consistently. (Respondent 7)

> Discussion with colleagues is valuable, in a supportive atmosphere.

> The meetings provide an opportunity to discuss ideas and refine thinking. This can then be shared with your own staff. (Respondent 9)

Facilitators' enthusiasm and developing expertise was a key factor in driving forward the continued development of CL in the schools, which was in turn supported by the group as a PLC.

The extent of the use of CL

Observations were carried out in seven classrooms in different schools (Jolliffe 2011) and they demonstrated in all cases that the skills of cooperating were developing. Pupils revealed a strong willingness to share in groups and they were observed mentoring each other.

Pupils in focus group interviews that followed the lesson observations frequently referred to 'helping each other' (27 times) when they worked in groups, demonstrating the value they placed on it. The majority of pupils found that being able to talk to a partner or team member helped their learning, as one secondary pupil (pupil C, interview 11 February 2009) said:

> Sometimes you don't understand the teacher's interpretation, but your friend might.

Pupils also felt that the use of roles in groups was helpful. As pupil B (interview 11 February 2009) said:

> I think when you are given different roles to do then it does actually make you do something.

They also clearly saw the importance of the teacher's role in organising this. Pupil D (interview 23 March 2009) commented on how the teacher:

> puts us with a partner so we can help each other …

Pupil B also commented (interview 11 February 2009):

> The way the teacher points it out as well because if they just say you are going to go into fours and puts in on the board, you won't really do it whereas Miss explains it all to us first so we all knew what we were doing and everything.

The use and value placed on CL was also verified by questionnaires to teachers in 2008 ($n = 97$) which showed that teachers were overwhelmingly positive about the impact of CL, in particular on pupils' social skills (all respondents strongly agreeing or agreeing that CL improves these skills). In relation to pupils' academic skills, a total of 91.8% of respondents agreed or strongly agreed that CL improves academic skills. A total of 92.8% of respondents agreed or strongly agreed that it improves pupils' attitudes to learning. Another significant aspect in the teachers' use of CL was their confidence in using it and analysis shows that 85.7% reported they were confident or very confident at using CL.

Observations in classrooms, interviews with pupils and questionnaires for teachers all verified that CL was becoming embedded across all schools. Whilst the network had proved fertile ground to develop this innovation, it was important to examine how this had been developed and whether it resonated with the research literature on factors in effective implementation.

Methods of implementation

Three main sources of evidence contribute to an overall understanding of how teachers in this case study were supported in implementing CL over the period from 2004 to 2009. These were questionnaires for teachers, minutes of termly facilitators' meetings and annual facilitators' surveys.

Questionnaires asked teachers to identify the length/type of training provided and what further support they required. Responses indicated that 74.2% had received in-house support and when asked what further type of support almost the same percentage reported they would like more of this, specifically support from the facilitator who 'is full of ideas and very enthusiastic' (Respondent 58).

Minutes of termly meetings showed that these predominately related to the support for staff in implementing and developing CL and the extensive resources that were produced collaboratively, including a staff handbook and a resources disk provided for all schools. The facilitator network meetings provided useful opportunities to up-skill facilitators, who in turn could support teachers in schools either individually or through regular staff training sessions and other forms of coaching.

Facilitators also completed an annual survey indicating progress in using CL in their schools. This indicated the on-going staff training and the role of the facilitator in providing this and supporting staff. In addition, there was a growing use of co-coaching and each year a proportion of staff were provided time to observe other teachers.

The network and impact on implementation

The literature on successful implementation of CL indicates a series of steps as discussed earlier. The importance of understanding how CL supports learning and reconciling this to existing beliefs and experiencing it in training was a necessary starting point. These aspects are difficult to verify from this study; however what is clear is that the gradual implementation supported by in-house experts was crucial. Working alongside teachers, team-teaching and coaching them provided teachers with the confidence to use CL. Over five years, it was clearly a long-term and sustained project, strongly backed by headteachers. What was perhaps unique about this study was the PLC of facilitators from each school all with a shared focus on CL.

This network demonstrated many of the features highlighted from research into effective networks as previously cited (Cordingley et al. 2006; Earl et al. 2006; Lieberman 1999). These features are not only crucial to the successful development of networks and PLCs generally, but they are also at the very heart of sustaining CL. One of the key elements is a shared focus and purpose in order to drive forward any innovation. For this network, a clear commitment to CL was evident and headteachers interviewed discussed the importance of a shared vision, for example, as Headteacher 5 commented:

LEARNING TO LEARN TOGETHER

We wrote an area action plan. We did a policy together, we pooled our community use funding.

A further important aspect is extensive collaboration and all headteachers and facilitators interviewed identified the importance of having a 'forum for sharing' and Headteacher 10 noted it was: 'all of us working for the benefit of us all'. The level of commitment by leaders is highlighted in the research literature into networks and was again evident here. Headteacher 6 acknowledged the importance of: 'the shared understanding, the shared viewpoint of what we are trying to achieve across the patch'.

A further important factor that is identified in the literature into effective networks is the mixture of information sharing and psychological support provided. The frequency of references to sharing and support shows this was also a significant factor here. Headteacher 4, for example, commented:

> Being able to pick up a phone, especially when I became acting Head and suddenly you thought, well I don't know how to do this and you felt confident to phone somebody on the patch and say I'm totally stuck.

Perhaps the most crucial aspect that made a significant difference to this network was the facilitator, or in-house expert. Whilst other research into networks acknowledges this, here, the facilitators became the lynchpin. They provided invaluable support coaching teachers in their schools, as teachers acknowledged in questionnaire responses. In turn, the facilitators were supported by working in a PLC of facilitators from each school and as Facilitator 3 commented: 'The opportunity to work alongside likeminded colleagues has been invaluable'.

Conclusion

As the foregoing has demonstrated, CL requires a sustained and collaborative process in order to implement it effectively. The case study discussed provides an example of bridging the gap between its potential and use through creating a network of schools working together, supported by a PLC of facilitators to provide in-house support.

The demand for schools working together in partnership and the development of PLCs within schools is gaining momentum internationally (DuFour et al. 2010; Hadfield and Jopling 2012; Lieberman 2012). What the empirical research here indicates is that both developing effective networks of schools and PLCs takes time, trust and effective relationships. Just as implementing CL is not a quick fix, neither is the development of PLCs. It is somewhat ironic that governments internationally in a drive for rapid school improvement see the panacea as something that is far from rapid.

This case study examined the particular features of one network that had been built up over a considerable period of time and the web of support it provided that enabled the effective implementation of CL. Whilst this is complex to put into practice, it requires schools to establish mutually supportive PLCs to be successful and sustained. Cooperation between pupils in the classroom, between teachers in schools for professional development, and between schools in networks and alliances builds slowly as the skills to work together develop. It can be worth the effort as this case study has shown, in bridging the gap between the potential and the reality of CL.

References

Baines, E., P. Blatchford, and P. Kutnick. 2003. "Changes in Grouping Practices Over Primary and Secondary School." *International Journal of Educational Research* 39 (1/2): 9–34.

LEARNING TO LEARN TOGETHER

Baines, E., P. Blatchford, and R. Webster. 2015. "The Challenges of Implementing Group-work in Primary School Classrooms and Including Pupils with special educational needs." *Education 3–13* 43 (1): 15–29.

Bassey, M. 1999. *Case Study Research in Educational Settings*. Buckingham: OU Press.

Blatchford, P., M. Galton, P. Kutnick, and E. Baines. 2005. *Improving the Effectiveness of Pupil Groups in Classrooms*. ESRC End of Research Report, Ref: L139 25 1046. Accessed February 8, 2006. http://www.spring-project.org.uk

Blatchford, P., P. Kutnick, E. Baines, and M. Galton. 2003. "Toward a Social Pedagogy of Classroom Group Work." *International Journal of Educational Research* 39 (1–2): 153–172.

Bolam, R., A. McMahon, L. Stoll, S. Thomas, M. Wallace, A. Greenwood, K. Hawkey, M. Ingram, A. Atkinson, and M. Smith. 2005. *Creating and Sustaining Effective Professional Learning Communities*. Research Report No. 637. London: Department for Education and Skills.

Bottery, M., and N. Wright. 2000. *Teachers and the State: Towards a Directed Profession*. London: Routledge.

Brody, C. M. 1992. "Cooperative Learning and Teacher Beliefs. A Constructivist View." Paper presented at the meeting of the International Association for the Study of Cooperation in Education, Utrecht, The Netherlands.

Brody, C. M. 1998. "The Significance of Teacher Beliefs for Professional Development ad Cooperative Learning." In *Professional Development for Cooperative Learning: Issues and Approaches*, edited by C. M. Brody and N. Davidson, 25–48. Albany: State University of New York Press.

Brody, C. 2004. "The Instructional Design of Cooperative Learning for Teacher Education." In *Teaching Cooperative Learning: The Challenge for Teacher Education*, edited by E. G. Cohen, C. M. Brody, and M. Shapon-Shevin, 185–194. Albany: State University of New York Press.

Brody, C. M., and N. Davidson, eds. 1998. *Professional Development for Cooperative Learning: Issues and Approaches*. Albany: State University of New York Press.

Cohen, E. 1994. *Designing Groupwork: Strategies for the Heterogeneous Classroom*. 2nd ed. New York: Teachers College Press.

Cooper, C., and J. Boyd. 1998. "Creating Sustained Professional Growth Through Collaborative Reflection." In *Professional Development for Cooperative Learning: Issues and Approaches*, edited by C. M. Brody and N. Davidson, 49–62. Albany: State University of New York Press.

Cordingley, P., A. Firth, E. King, and H. Mitchell. 2006. *Systematic Research Review: The Impact of Networks on Pupils, Practitioners, Organisations and the Communities They Serve*. Nottingham, National College for School Leadership. Accessed August 23, 2009. http://networkedlearning.ncsl.org.uk/collections/network-research-series/summaries/understanding-learning-networks.pdf

Decuyper, S., F. Dochy, and P. Van den Bossche. 2010. "Grasping the Dynamic Complexity of Team Learning. An Integrative Systemic Model for Effective Team Learning in Organisations." *Educational Research Review* 5: 111–133.

Deutsch, M. 1949. "A Theory of Cooperation and Competition." *Human Relations* 2 (2): 129–152.

Dewey, J. 1916. *Democracy and Education*. New York: Macmillan.

DuFour, R., R. DuFour, R. Eaker, and T. Many. 2010. *Learning by Doing: A Handbook for Professional Learning Communities at Work*. 2nd ed. Bloomington, IN: Solution Tree Press.

Earl, L., S. Katz, S. Elgie, S. Ben Jafaar, L. Foster, P. Sammons, and T. Mujtaba. 2006. *How Networked Learning Communities Work* (External Evaluation Phase 3). Toronto: Aporio Consulting.

Feger, S., and E. Arruda. 2008. *Professional Learning Communities: Key Themes from the Literature*. The Education Alliance, Brown University. Accessed March 24, 2013. www.alliance.brown.edu

Galton, M., and L. Hargreaves. 2009. "Group Work: Still a Neglected Art?" *Cambridge Journal of Education* 39 (1): 1–6.

Gillies, R. M. 2003. "Structuring Cooperative Group Work in Classrooms." *International Journal of Educational Research* 39 (1–2): 35–49.

Gillies, R. 2008. "The Effects of Cooperative Learning on Junior High School Students' Behaviours, Discourse, and Learning During a Science-Based Learning Activity." *School Psychology International* 29 (3): 328–347.

Gillies, R. M., and M. Boyle. 2010. "Teachers' Reflections on Cooperative Learning: Issues of Implementation." *Teaching and Teacher Education* 26 (4): 933–940.

Hadfield, M., and M. Jopling. 2012. "School Networks, Networked Learning and Network Theory." In *The Routledge International Handbook of Teacher and School Development*, edited by C. Day, 516–526. Abingdon: Routledge.

Hargreaves, A., and M. Fullan. 2012. *Professional Capital: Transforming Teaching in Every School*. Toronto, Ontario, Canada: Teachers College Press.

Harris, A., and M. Jones. 2011. *Professional Learning Communities in Action*. London: Leannta.

Hattie, J. 2009. *Visible Learning: A Synthesis of over 800 Meta-Analyses Relating to Achievement*. London: Routledge.

Hord, S. M. 1997. *Professional Learning Communities: Communities of Continuous Inquiry and Improvement*. Austin, TX: Southwest Educational Development Laboratory.

Jenkins, J., L. Antil, S. Wayne, and P. Vadasy. 2003. "How Cooperative Learning Works for Special Education and Remedial Students." *Exceptional Children* 69 (3): 279–292.

Johnson, D. W., and R. T. Johnson. 1975. *Learning Together and Alone: Cooperative, Competitive and Individualistic Learning*. Needham Heights, MA: Allyn and Bacon.

Johnson, D. W., and R. Johnson. 1989. *Cooperation and Competition: Theory and Research*. Edina, MN: Interaction Book.

Johnson, D. W., and R. Johnson. 1994. *Leading the Cooperative School*. 2nd ed. Edina, MN: Interaction Book.

Johnson, D. W., and R. T. Johnson. 1996. "Conflict Resolution and Peer Mediation Programmes in Elementary and Secondary Schools: A Review of the Research." *Review of Educational Research* 66 (4): 459–506.

Johnson, D., and R. Johnson. 1998. "Effective Staff Development in Cooperative Learning: Training, Transfer, and Long-Term Use." In *Professional Development for Cooperative Learning: Issues and Approaches*, edited by C. M. Brody and N. Davidson, 223–242. Albany: State University of New York Press.

Johnson, D. W., and F. P. Johnson. 2000. *Joining Together: Group Theory and Group Skills*. 6th ed. Boston, MA: Allyn and Bacon.

Johnson, D. W., Roger T. Johnson, and E. Holubec. 1998. *Cooperation in the Classroom*. Boston: Allyn and Bacon.

Jolliffe, W. 2011. "Co-operative Learning: Making It Work in the Classroom." *Journal of Co-operative Studies* 44 (3): 31–42.

Jolliffe, W., and H. Hutchinson. 2007. "Implementing Cooperative Learning in a Networked Learning Community." *Education 3–13* 35 (1): 5–16.

Kagan, S. 1994. *Cooperative Learning*. San Juan Capistrano, CA: Kagan Cooperative Learning.

Katz, S., and L. Earl. 2010. "Learning about Networked Learning Communities." *School Effectiveness and School Improvement* 21 (1): 27–51.

Kennedy, A. 2005. "Models of Continuing Professional Development: A Framework for Analysis." *Journal of In-service Education* 31 (2): 235–250.

Kutnick, P., S. Hodgkinson, J. Sebba, S. Humphreys, M. Galton, S. Steward, P. Blatchford, and E. Baines. 2007. *Pupil Grouping Strategies and Practices at Key Stage 2 and 3*. Research Report 796. Nottingham: DfES.

Kyndt, E., E. Raes, B. Lismont, F. Timmers, E. Cascallar, and F. Dochy. 2013. "A Meta-Analysis of the Effects of Face-to-Face Cooperative Learning. Do Recent Studies Falsify or Verify Earlier Findings?" *Educational Research Review* 10: 133–149.

Lave, J., and E. Wenger. 1991. *Situated Learning: Legitimate Peripheral Participation*. New York: Cambridge University Press.

Lewin, K. 1948. *Resolving Social Conflicts*. New York: Harper.

Lieberman, A. J. 1999. "Networks." *Journal of Staff Development* 20 (3). Accessed May 26, 2014. http://networkedlearning.ncsl.org.uk/knowledge-base/think-pieces/networks-lieberman-2005.pdf

Lieberman, A. 2012. "Learning about Professional Communities: Their Practices, Problems and Possibilities." In *The Routledge International Handbook of Teacher and School Development*, edited by C. Day, 469–475. Abingdon: Routledge.

McLaughlin, M., and J. Talbert. 2006. *Building School-Based Teacher Learning Communities: Professional Strategies to Improve Student Achievement*. New York, NY: Teachers College Press.

NCSL. 2007. *Networked Learning Communities*. National College of School Leadership. Accessed December 11, 2007. www.ncsl.org.uk/nlc

NCSL. 2012. *Powerful Professional Learning: A School Leader's Guide to Joint Practice Development*. Nottingham: NCSL.

Rolheiser, C., and L. Stevahn. 1998. "The Role of Staff Developers in Promoting Effective Teacher Decision-Making." In *Professional Development for Cooperative Learning: Issues and Approaches*, edited by C. M. Brody and N. Davidson, 63–78. Albany: State University of New York Press.

Roy, P. 1998. "Staff Development that Makes a Difference." In *Professional Development for Cooperative Learning: Issues and Approaches*, edited by C. M. Brody and N. Davidson, 79–99. Albany: NY: State University of New York Press.

Schmuck, R. 1998. "Mutually-Sustaining Relationships Between Organisation Development and Cooperative Learning." In *Professional Development for Cooperative Learning: Issues and Approaches*, edited by C. M. Brody and N. Davidson, 243–254. Albany: State University of New York Press.

Schmuck, R., and P. Schmuck. 2001. *Group Processes in the Classroom*. 8th ed. Boston: McGraw Hill.

Sebba, J., P. Kent, and J. Tregenza. 2010. *Joint Practice Development: What Does the Evidence Suggest Are Effective Approaches?* Nottingham: National College of School Leadership (NCSL).

Sharan, S. 1990. *Cooperative Learning: Theory and Research*. Westport, CN: Praeger.

Sharan, Y. 2010. "Cooperative Learning for Academic and Social Gains: Valued Pedagogy, Problematic Practice." *European Journal of Education* 45 (2): 300–313.

Sharan, Y., and S. Sharan. 1992. *Expanding Cooperative Learning Through Group Investigation*. New York: Teachers College Press.

Sharan, Y., and S. Sharan. 1994. "Group Investigation in the Cooperative Classroom." In *Handbook of Cooperative Learning Methods*, edited by S. Sharan, 97–114. Westport, CT: Praeger.

Slavin, R. E. 1995. *Cooperative Learning: Theory, Research, and Practice*. Boston: Allyn and Bacon.

Slavin, R. 1996. *Education for All*. Lisse: Swets and Zeitlinger.

Slavin, R. E. 2015. "Cooperative Learning in Elementary Schools." *Education 3–13* 43 (1): 5–14.

Stevahn, L. J., R. Johnson, K. Oberle, and L. Wahl. 2000. "Effects of Conflict Resolution Training Integrated into a Kindergarten Curriculum." *Child Development* 71: 772–784.

Stoll, L., R. Bolam, A. McMahon, M. Wallace, and S. Thomas. 2006. "Professional Learning Communities: A Review of the Literature." *Journal of Educational Change* 7: 221–258.

Wenger, E. 1998. *Communities of Practice: Learning, Meaning and Identity*. Cambridge: Cambridge University Press.

Yin, R. 2009. *Case Study Research: Design and Methods*. Applied Social Research Methods Series. 4th ed. London: Sage.

Meaningful learning in the cooperative classroom

Yael Sharan

GRIP, Group Investigation projects, Tel Aviv, Israel

> Meaningful learning is based on more than what teachers transmit; it promotes the construction of knowledge out of learners' experience, feelings and exchanges with other learners. This educational view is based on the constructivist approach to learning and the co-operative learning approach. Researchers and practitioners in various countries and settings seek ways to incorporate these approaches to create meaningful learning in the multicultural classroom and in the co-operative learning classroom. This article presents some of the ideas, studies and methods that signal a major shift of emphasis in education from product to process.

Introduction

Twenty children in the third grade class sat in rows, two to a table, in a dusty farming village in Israel in 1954. All were recent immigrants: some from Kurdistan, some from Iran, and a few from the Karaite community in Egypt. Each child was one of many in a family. Their parents were preoccupied with the hardships of learning how to be farmers so that they could make a living.

This was my first teaching post and as a novice teacher I was confident in what I knew: the traditional transmission approach to teaching. I dutifully set out to follow the routine that treats all students as one group, with me as teacher–leader who assigns texts related to the prescribed curriculum, instructs, or demonstrates to the whole class, assigns some form of individual practice (homework) and organises individual assessment (tests).

Very quickly I came to realise what I did not know. The glazed looks on the students' faces, the frequent disruptions and the erratic attendance were unavoidable indications that I did not know how to capture the children's attention and interest. Then one day, when teaching (or rather talking) about the sun's distance from the earth, one girl called out: 'I get it! The sun is as far from the earth as Iran is from Israel!'

That was the turning point in my teaching. The girl's remark made me realise that my job was not to continue the traditional one-way communication from teacher to students by being a 'banker' (to borrow Paolo Freire's term), who 'deposits' knowledge without taking time to explore the students' minds, but to bridge the gap between their world and the curriculum.

LEARNING TO LEARN TOGETHER

From then I made concerted efforts to learn how to guide my students to use their own world as bridges to learning. They told me stories about their lives, taught me words and songs in their first languages, and created reading material that grew out of their interests, experiences and knowledge, all of which became an integral part of the learning process. Luckily I lived in the village and knew the students' families. Over many cups of mint tea we exchanged stories about our customs, aspirations and frustrations. In school, I was guided in my choice of procedures (too early in my teaching career to call them methods or theories, even with a small 't') by my desire to connect the curriculum to the students' lives. Theories with a capital T did not constrain my choice of teaching methods. I had no idea that this was a 'multicultural classroom and had not yet heard of small group teaching, (the term 'cooperative learning' (CL) had not been coined yet) or even of individualised learning.

One source of validation of these efforts in that dusty village came several years later from Sylvia Ashton-Warner's book 'Teacher' (1963), the moving account of her efforts to teach reading to her young Maori and English students in New Zealand by using their inner world as bridges to learning. By being wholeheartedly attentive to the children's *words* she helped them create reading material that grew out of their *world* and replaced texts used to teach reading at the time like 'Come John come. Come and look' (36), which were far removed from Maori children's volatile lives and even from the English children's more reserved lives. Ashton-Warner was a pioneer in creating meaningful teaching procedures; her deep-seated humanism paralleled the lessons emerging at the time from the human sciences.

The reality of our situation propelled me to teach in ways that were further validated by what I later learned from contemporary research and theories of teaching in general, and of teaching in the heterogeneous and multicultural classroom in particular. This experience initiated my lifelong quest for ways to make learning meaningful to all learners in the complex reality of a classroom. Many of the discoveries along the way were made through collaboration with colleagues in the fields of co-operative learning and multicultural education. What follows is an attempt to present the ideas, studies and methods of but a few of the more inspiring researchers and practitioners that I have encountered over time.

Meaningful learning

In the second half of the twentieth century several influential concepts were taking hold that led to new understandings of cognitive development and served as the foundation of two major approaches to learning and teaching: constructivism and co-operative learning. Both approaches sought to actively engage all students in learning and signalled a shift of emphasis in teaching from product and content to process. More and more educators and educational psychologists realised that the fact that a teacher presents information to students, or asks them to read a passage from a book, does not transform the content into knowledge. They viewed knowledge as what learners construct out of elements of information, feelings and experience, and exchanges with other learners, not something that exists in chunks in the external world to be swallowed whole (Sigel and Cocking 1977).

Instructional conversations

A substantial application of the constructivist approach to teaching and learning is the design of 'Instructional Conversations' (IC) by Tharp and Gallimore (1988, 1991). Their

LEARNING TO LEARN TOGETHER

model of teacher-guided conversations with small groups of students calls for teachers to ask questions, not to elicit answers they have in mind but to enable children to express and clarify their understanding of academic content, based on their knowledge and experiences. As Goldenberg explains (1991, 1), 'the teacher encourages expression of students' own ideas, builds upon information students provide and experiences they have had, and guides students to increasingly sophisticated levels of understanding'.

IC take off from the student's zone of proximal development, (the level of cognitive development at which he or she cannot complete a task, understand an issue or solve a problem alone), then build on it to further develop skills of understanding and interpretation (Vygotsky 1978). Children benefit from sharing their understanding with the teacher and with fellow students in a climate that encourages expression of and respect for diverse viewpoints. Learning how students negotiate meaning facilitates teachers' efforts to plan how to continue to support their students' learning. While IC are not considered a co-operative learning model per se they are most compatible with the basic principles of CL, as we shall see later in this article.

Since language is the vehicle of IC it is understandable that their underlying principles and procedures have been applied to the study and practice of teaching and learning a second or foreign language and to literacy in general, especially with minority children (Goldenberg 1991). Such was the case in a study of one teacher's implementation of IC that led to a change in her approach to the teaching of reading (O'Bryan 1999). As the teacher became skilled in guiding IC there was a gradual shift in her teaching from recitation to full engagement of her students in the process of learning. The change in her pupils' learning patterns was convincing; they gave longer responses, initiated conversations and learned to contribute to, challenge and extend each other's statements. An offshoot of IC is the experience-text-relationship method that uses discussion to link what the child already knows to what she or he will be reading (Au 1979).

IC grew out of Tharp and Gallimore's studies of the socio-linguistic patterns of Native American nations and of various ethnic groups in Hawaii whose language patterns and learning styles were in contrast with the teachers' language patterns and transmission style of teaching. Their work inspired the consideration of broader changes in the teaching of all groups with similar cultural discontinuity (Goldenberg 1991; Tharp and Yamauchi 1994), and was also applied to efforts at school-wide change (Saunders and Goldenberg 2005). A more recent application is the five-year professional development project for teachers and administrators in a network of Jewish parochial schools in Florida called 'Building Relationships through Conversations' (Lambert and Mitrani 2013). By giving each participant an equal voice and structuring norms for the exchange of views and ideas, the conversations created shared understanding, increased trust, instructional leadership and above all, sustained relationships.

Meaningful learning in the multicultural classroom

The findings from Tharp and Gallimore's research highlight the failure and frustration experienced by children whose socio-linguistic backgrounds are different from those of their teachers. In such cases, students and teachers often have conflicting expectations of what and how learning should take place in school (Au and Kawakami 1994; Tharp and Gallimore 1988, 1991). This is particularly evident today in the growing number of classrooms with students of diverse ethnic, cultural, religious and economic backgrounds. Turkish children in Danish classrooms, Albanian children in Italian classrooms, Russian children in Greek classrooms, Chinese students in New Zealand universities, these are but a few examples of the dramatic change in the composition of the student body in today's classrooms. Literacy patterns that children grow up with are part of the familiar and valued aspects of their identity. If teachers insist that students adopt unfamiliar language patterns, they may be threatening students' core identities (Hedegaard 2003), and increase their feelings of alienation from school.

In response to this pervasive reality, teacher educators have become more aware of the need for teachers to acquire intercultural awareness. Teachers of a second or foreign language, for example, are encouraged to make intercultural communication and dialogue part of their teaching through lesson designs that enable all students to speak and share their experiences (Magos and Simopoulos 2009). There are also increasing efforts to instil an appreciation for diversity in teacher education through international field experiences and cultural exchange that are more than tours of foreign cultures. The programme includes in-depth discussions and reflection on participants' own world views and strives to develop their ability to interact sensitively and competently in cultural contexts other than their own. These experiences focus on participating teachers' perceptions of 'otherness' and seek to broaden their perspectives of human differences (Walters, Garii, and Walters 2009).

For today's diverse classrooms, Banks (1991) recommends expanding the construction of knowledge beyond the individual student's process of making sense of the world to the understanding of the implicit cultural assumptions and frames of reference in curricular materials. When teachers encourage students to question and investigate the implicit perspectives and values in various sources, they enable students to become critical learners and develop better understanding of how historians, scientists and others construct *their* 'knowledge'. Making sense of the world, of the classroom and of various sources of information involves negotiating multiple interpretations, 'not only in your own head but also with the heads of others, who all have unique backgrounds and ways of constructing meaning' (Hammerberg 2004, 650).

An instructive example of efforts to make learning more meaningful and to increase school success in multicultural classrooms is a three-year study of Aboriginal and non-Aboriginal high school students in a western Canadian city (Kanu 2007). One teacher made successful attempts to integrate aspects of Aboriginal cultural knowledge, perspectives and sources into the social studies curriculum. By using various methods that were familiar to the students, such as expressing their ideas in drawings or poetry, and creating discussion circles or problem-solving circles, the teacher reduced the cultural discontinuity between students' homes and school. Students were motivated by the teacher's knowledge of Aboriginal culture and content, his positive attitude towards them and his clear desire to have them do well. By including Aboriginal sources in the curriculum, he avoided what Sleeter (2012) calls

the tendency to view culturally responsive pedagogy as cultural celebration that is disconnected from academic learning ... (where) learning 'about' culture ... substitutes for learning to teach challenging academic knowledge and skills through the cultural processes and knowledge students bring to school with them. (569)

Another welcome outcome of this intervention was the benefit to non-Aboriginal students in the class. Kanu reports that one non-Aboriginal student remarked that

the circle discussions had helped him experience a level of cognitive dissonance from, and uneasiness with, some stereotypical views he had carried about Aboriginal peoples. This in turn had enabled him to develop new perspectives on stereotyping and a better understanding of his north-end Aboriginal neighbors. (2007, 38)

We may assume that the teacher in this study also acquired new perspectives about his students. It seems that he took a significant step in developing the basic components of cultural competence: knowledge (of how different cultural groups understand the world); skills (in handling classroom interaction to facilitate equitable learning) and disposition (open-minded attitudes and respect for diverse world views) (Mushi 2004, 184). Although modest in scope this study reinforces Ogbu's admonition that teachers need to learn about and understand students' culture and history to better appreciate how they affect students' school orientations and behaviours (1992).

Researchers worldwide continue to be concerned with students' and teachers' efforts to bridge any mismatch between the students' culture and the cultural model of the teacher and the school. Whether studying the effects of a teaching experiment in New York City with Puerto Rican children or in Denmark with young Palestinian boys, the aim is to create meaningful teaching that helps students acquire skills and knowledge in a learning environment that strengthens their personal identities and enables them to accept both their cultural background and the society in which they live (Hedegaard 2003). There are multiple suggestions for educational interventions in such classrooms that strive to turn them into *inter*cultural learning communities, where teachers consider both differences and similarities and create opportunities for contact and interaction among students (Portera 2008). When teachers join their students in the process and both become learners, the classroom becomes a fully intercultural one; ' ... the teacher and students learn together, share their cultures and construct new knowledge in the classroom' (Banks 1991, 138).

The collaboration between student and teacher and between student and student in efforts to make learning meaningful creates an engaged classroom where students ask questions, share ideas and understanding, and construct meaningful knowledge. These are among the outstanding features of co-operative learning methods, models and procedures, as elaborated in the following section.

How CL creates meaningful learning

Since the 1960s CL has grown to be an 'umbrella' pedagogy that generates a diversified body of methods, models and instructional procedures with increasingly diverse applications. Many ways of organising a CL classroom raise the question of what they all have in common. Brody and Davidson (1998) offer a succinct and helpful definition: CL methods, models and instructional procedures organise students to:

> work in groups toward a common goal or outcome
> or share a common problem or task,
> in such a way that they can only succeed in completing the work
> through behaviour that demonstrates interdependence,
> while holding individual contributions and efforts accountable (8).

This definition integrates the principal elements that emanate from the main theories that contribute to making CL what it is today. Regardless of their theoretical orientation researchers of CL have consistently combined research with the development and design of classroom and school action plans that include the elements in the above definition.

Researchers have also turned their attention to teacher education for CL (Cohen, Brody, and Sapon-Shavon 2004). While there is no one way to teach teachers how to implement CL, there is general consensus that experiential learning is an essential feature of any programme that seeks to help teachers move from the transmission model, where they impart prescribed facts and ideas, to the transaction model that invites students to actively participate in the learning process and beyond the transformation model (Brody 1998; Sharan 2010). Learning *about* CL alone cannot bring about the necessary change in teachers' perception of their role in CL (Koutselini 2008/2009).

Underlying theories of co-operative learning and their application

CL was never a uniform, homogeneous approach to teaching and learning; it was born to several 'parents' who nurtured it with complementary theories. Together they provided a powerful rationale as to why CL successfully promotes academic and social skills and contributes to meaningful learning. Following are brief descriptions of a few of the major theories and their application to CL.

The philosopher and psychologist John Dewey, for one, advocated learning in a social context, in which there is free communication and interchange of ideas about the curriculum, and where learners have a say in what and how they will learn (Dewey 1899/1943). In the second half of the twentieth century Dewey's view of education, together with the constructivist theory of cognitive development, inspired the development of the co-operative learning model of Group Investigation (GI) (Thelen 1981; Sharan and Sharan 1992).

GI calls for learners to raise questions about a topic and together with their peers seek answers to these questions and shape their findings into meaningful constructs. At first small groups of learners plan what they will study and how they will study, and thus largely determine the content of their inquiry. As the investigation progresses, students divide the responsibilities for various aspects of the investigation, combining individual, pair and group learning. When they complete their inquiry group members integrate and summarise their findings and present them to their classmates. Throughout the process teachers guide their students in the appropriate interpersonal and learning skills. Other systematic models of inquiry-based learning, such as problem-based learning, share the basic educational premises of this approach to co-operative learning (Hmelo-Silver, Duncan, and Clark 2007; Sharan, Sharan, and Tan 2013).

Whereas Dewey can be seen as the philosopher of an active inquiry approach to learning, the prominent social psychologist Kurt Lewin (1947) contributed to the shaping of the interpersonal dimensions of CL. Like Dewey, Lewin believed that learning is more effective when it is an active rather than a passive process, and when pursued collaboratively. Applying the effective management of group relationships in the classroom maximises their positive influence on the learning process (Schmuck and Schmuck 1971/2001), which are applicable to all forms of co-operative learning, and compatible with all theoretical orientations.

Another significant 'parent' of CL was the social psychologist Morton Deutsch (1949) whose extensive research demonstrated that groups are more productive when members are co-operative rather than competitive in their relationships. Through the communication of ideas, coordination of efforts, friendliness and pride in one's group, co-operation, as opposed to competition, increases the groups' effectiveness in reaching its goals (Schmuck 2010). Deutsch conceptualised the principle of social interdependence. The way social interdependence is structured determines the way persons interact and determines the outcomes of their interaction (Johnson, Johnson, and Holubec 1998). Social or positive interdependence is the basic element in all CL methods and procedures: group members depend on one another to carry out learning assignments; they bring together diverse strengths, interests, capacities, experiences, knowledge, perspectives and personalities to reach learning outcomes that surpass those that can be achieved by individual members. They also depend on one another for personal and social support.

Learning Together, the model of co-operative learning based on Deutsch's theory and research was developed and is continuously researched by David Johnson, Roger Johnson and colleagues at the University of Minnesota. At the heart of the model are the following five elements they have established as crucial for effective CL: positive interdependence, promotive interaction, individual accountability, interpersonal and small-group social skills, and group processing. In Learning Together, teachers design assignments and choose materials based on the academic and social objectives they set, determine group size, choose a way of assigning students to groups and assign group roles (Johnson, Johnson, and Holubec 1998). Among the additional procedures developed and researched by the Johnsons and their colleagues are informal co-operative learning, co-operative base groups and creative controversy (Johnson and Johnson 2009).

An additional part of the theoretical mosaic that constitutes the CL approach is the motivational perspective of Robert Slavin (1999), which serves as the foundation for co-operative methods that include team rewards, individual accountability and equal opportunities for success. One application of this theory is STAD (Student Teams-Achievement Divisions) developed by Slavin and colleagues at Johns Hopkins University, which is a way of organising classroom learning to effectively teach well-defined objectives in a wide variety of subjects. In STAD, students work together to learn specific content: each is responsible for his or her learning as well as for team mates' learning. Its unique emphasis is on 'the use of team goals and team success, which can only be achieved if all team members learn the objectives being taught' (3); team rewards motivate students to help one another to learn as best they can. Slavin and Madden (2009) have expanded their research and its application through the Success for All Foundation. The Foundation offers a comprehensive school reform model that incorporates CL principles in the restructuring of curriculum, instruction, professional development and accommodations for children who have learning difficulties.

A sociological approach to co-operative learning developed by Elizabeth Cohen (1994) focuses on the effects of status characteristics and expectations on group interaction. Status characteristics (e.g. social ranking, reading ability) serve to shape the group's expectations of how well an individual group member will perform. Low-status group members may barely be heard; high-status students may constantly influence a group, sometimes beyond the actual quality of their contribution.

To address the issue of unequal status in groups that results in unequal influence on, and participation in the completion of a co-operative task Cohen and colleagues at Stanford University developed the CL model Complex Instruction (CI). The CI model stresses that no one student will have all the abilities to carry out a learning assignment, but each will have some of the requisite abilities. The CI team has adapted existing curricular material so that learning tasks involve students' multiple abilities and assign competencies to low-status students. Learning tasks are challenging and open-ended, without one specific solution, so that students can explore various solutions and examine them from different perspectives, based on their varying abilities and backgrounds.

Gleaning from the major theoretical foundations of CL, Spencer Kagan's Structural Approach presents over 200 content-free ways of structuring group interaction (Kagan and Kagan 2009). Each Structure consists of a sequence of steps that guides students to interact according to specific co-operative behaviours and for various learning goals. The Structures are ways to maximise the basic CL elements as formulated by this approach: positive interdependence, individual accountability, equal participation and simultaneous interaction. Structures may be used repeatedly in any content area and one or more times in a lesson and can often be used together with other CL models.

The CL methods and models summarised above and others call for teachers to develop students' social and communication skills and to monitor how groups work together. After groups complete a learning assignment teachers guide them in the process of reflection on how they worked together to achieve their goal and how they can improve the way they work together.

The various CL methods and models emphasise different CL components but neverthe-less are not mutually exclusive. In fact they can be seen as a continuum based on the degree of freedom group members have in choosing what and how they will learn. The less struc-ture and direction the teacher provides the more freedom of choice students have. Many teachers introduce CL into their classrooms by using highly organised Structures and STAD when teaching prescribed curricula, thus changing the *way* material is learned without altering the material itself (Rapport 2004). In the less teacher directed models, such as CI and GI, teachers tailor co-operative learning specifically to their students' inter-ests and needs. In these models, not all the learning material may be learned co-operatively, but those that are – that present a multifaceted problem that has more than one answer and/or more than one source for the answer – either altered accordingly by the teacher (in CI) or constructed by the students (in GI). In both these models, groups do not always have iden-tical assignments and the final outcome of the groups' learning cannot be specified in advance; the quantity and pace of learning depends a great deal on the students' capabilities and preparedness for this type of learning. CI, GI and the other CL methods, models and procedures may be used repeatedly and in varying sequences, depending on the degree of appropriate co-operative social and learning skill students and teachers have acquired.

CL practice continues to be supported by research that examines its effectiveness under different conditions and subject matter, and constantly revises and refines both co-operative learning theory and practice (Johnson and Johnson 2009; Slavin 2010, this issue). Researchers too numerous to mention here continue to examine the effects of the specific methods and of CL in general on achievement, social interaction, cognitive processes, motivation and school organisation. Also studied are the similarities and differences between methods; students' and teachers' perceptions of CL; the connections between CL procedures and methods and inclusion, group composition, size, discussion, task struc-ture, helping behaviours and teacher education for CL (Sharan 2012b). A recent study con-tributes to the ongoing discussion about the conditions under which group and individual rewards are most helpful for achieving effective CL (Buchs et al. 2011). Results suggest that when group members carry out a CL task that calls for them to exchange information they learn the same whether or not they are rewarded as a group. Additional areas of research in the past few decades are the application of CL to higher education (Cooper, Robinson and Ball 2009; Jimma and Gillies n.d.) and to the training of professionals in fields previously not studied, such as nursing, business, engineering and music, among others (Baloche 2011; Sharan 2012a).

Meaningful learning in the co-operative learning classroom

When you enter a CL classroom you see students sitting in pairs or in small groups of three or four, and, depending on the design and goal of the CL method, model or procedure employed, you will hear them talking for a variety of purposes: to help one another learn, to explain and share ideas, to share materials, to solve problems or to plan how to carry out a learning assignment. How do such interactive behaviours take hold in the classroom? What does the teacher have to learn to do? What do students learn to do?

An essential first step is for teachers to accept that even in a seemingly homogeneous class learning can be enhanced by learners' diverse ideas and knowledge. An effective way of enlisting these ideas is to enable learners to ask questions of one another and of the teacher. As we learned above from IC, learners' questions reveal their thought processes and the assumptions they bring to discussions of an idea, a topic or a way of solving a problem. By listening to students' questions teachers learn what students already know and what they want to know, which helps teachers connect learning to the students' world and capabilities so as to make learning meaningful for them.

In effect, teachers enter into a new 'contract' with their students: teachers ask questions that invite more than one answer, not to hear the answers *they* know but to listen non-judgementally and learn what the students know or think; students learn to trust that their contributions to learning have value. The teacher's respect for students' individual and collaborative voices encourages further participation and interaction in group and class-wide activities. Goldenberg (1991) and Watson (2001) offer many examples of how, by inviting students to express their own ideas and expand on them, teachers help students use what they know to construct new understanding. For a start, teachers may make one specific small change in their traditional practice by inquiring 'about students' understanding of concepts before sharing their own understanding of these concepts' (Watson 2001, 142). Teachers are often rewarded by hearing unexpected ideas from their students. Changing the role of questions is the first step in creating the open and accepting atmosphere in which a CL class can flourish.

Further evidence of the pivotal role that teachers' and students' questions play in co-operative learning comes from the extensive research by Gillies (2000, 2002, 2004, 2006) and colleagues, who thoroughly investigated the conditions that affect students' ability to ask questions as well as their ability to exercise thinking and problem-solving skills in CL tasks (Gillies and Boyle 2008; Gillies and Haynes 2011; Gillies and Khan 2009). They also studied how to effectively train teachers to use specific cognitive and meta-cognitive questions that challenge children's thinking, problem solving and reasoning during co-operative learning, all of which are vital to developing thinking and learning skills.

This body of empirical research highlights the centrality of the teacher's role in structuring learning in co-operative groups so that students gain the maximum benefits from working together. It also demonstrates the importance of training teachers in the types of mediated learning behaviours that challenge students' thinking and promote higher order thinking and reasoning. Results show that with appropriate training teachers learned to model questioning strategies in the classroom so that they could explicitly teach them to students for effective co-operation. Students in these studies asked more questions than their peers who did not benefit from this specific training and also learned to provide more detailed explanations and shorter responses (Gillies and Boyle 2008; Gillies and Haynes 2011). Moreover, when students were placed in situations where they were expected to work co-operatively and they were taught, both explicitly and implicitly, how to ask questions that challenge each other's thinking during their discussions, they became 'aware of the importance of providing elaborated and detailed responses that are helpful to their group mates' (Gillies and Khan 2009, 22).

To learn how teachers perceived CL, and how they perceived their students' responses to CL, Gillies and Boyle (2011) interviewed seven teachers who had implemented CL for two years. The data from the interviews illuminate teachers' perceptions of all the essential elements of CL, such as structuring groups, team work, interpersonal and communication skills, organising groups and group processing. Among teachers' comments, the following ones reveal how some understood the value of team work: ' ... I think it's really important for kids to learn to work in groups'; 'A lot of employers, I hear, are looking for the ability to negotiate, to compromise, to work as a team ... '; 'I think the big thing is the concept of interdependence because if ultimately we are looking at what we've done as a group ... we think that we couldn't have done it if everyone hadn't contributed' (68). Teachers said that they believed that their lessons were more interesting, the children learned more, they felt more confident and they themselves learned to work more closely with their colleagues. Teachers also noted that CL 'needed to be well planned, students needed to be prepared to work in groups, and teachers' expectations needed to be explicitly stated if the benefits attributed to CL were to be realized' (63).

There is no doubt that effective CL hinges on the well-planned design of the learning task assigned to students. Although there are many factors to take into account when designing a CL lesson or assignment, such as learning goals, cultural factors, the degree to which students and teachers are prepared for group work, group size and composition, the amount of time available, etc., there are some basic guidelines that ensure the interaction and interdependence that constitute a group-worthy task (Lotan 2003; Sharan and Sharan 1992):

(1) A clearly stated group goal that justifies two or more students learning together, often formulated as a question that generates more than one answer and/or has more than one resource for the answer.
(2) Directions that activate positive interdependence: dividing the task so that each student has a distinct part and can actively contribute to the completion of the task.
(3) Directions geared to the level of interpersonal skills group members have acquired and are comfortable with.
(4) Clear information about criteria for the evaluation of the learning content.
(5) A well-designed and executed CL assignment, lesson and/or project is essential for realising the promise of CL: the development of co-operative social, communication and learning skills that promote meaningful learning and teaching.

Last year there was a reunion of the first graduating class of the elementary school in the village where I began teaching. The village is no longer dusty and many of the graduates are now grandparents. At the reunion one woman came up to me and told me that she still remembers the poems and stories she learned in school. 'The poems and stories became part of me because you helped me connect them to the stories my parents used to tell me, which I loved so much'.

References

Ashton-Warner, S. 1963. *Teacher.* New York, NY: Simon and Schuster.
Au, K. 1979. "Using the Experience-Text-Relationship Method with Minority Children." *The Reading Teacher* 32 (6): 677–679.
Au, K. and A. Kawakami. 1994. "Cultural Congruence in Instruction." In *Teaching Diverse Populations,* edited by E. R. Hollins, J. E. King, and W. C. Hayman, 5–24. Albany, NY: SUNY.
Baloche, L. 2011. "A Brief View of Cooperative Learning from Across the Pond, Around the World, and Over Time." *Journal of Co-operative Studies* 44 (3): 25–30.
Banks, J. 1991. "Teaching Multicultural Literacy to Teachers." *Teaching Education* 4 (1): 135–142.

Brody, C. 1998. "The Significance of Teacher Beliefs for Professional Development and Cooperative Learning." In *Professional Development for Cooperative Learning: Issues and Approaches*, edited by Celeste Brody and Neil Davidson, 25–48. Albany, NY: SUNY.

Brody, C., and N. Davidson. 1998. "Introduction: Professional Development and Cooperative Learning." In *Professional Development for Cooperative Learning: Issues and Approaches*, edited by Celeste Brody and Neil Davidson, 3–24. Albany, NY: SUNY.

Buchs, C., I. Gilles, M. Dutrevis, and F. Butera. 2011. "Pressure to Cooperate: Is Positive Reward Interdependence Really Needed in Cooperative Learning?" *British Journal of Educational Psychology* 81 (1): 135–146.

Cohen, E. G. 1994. *Designing Groupwork: Strategies for the Heterogeneous Classroom*. 2nd ed. New York, NY: Teachers College.

Cohen, Elizabeth G., Celeste Brody, and Mara Sapon-Shavon, eds. 2004. *Teaching Cooperative Learning: The Challenge for Teacher Education*. Albany, NY: SUNY.

Cooper, J., P. Robinson, and D. Ball, eds. 2009. *Small Group Instruction in Higher Education: Lessons from the Past, Visions of the Future*. Oklahoma: New Forums Press.

Deutsch, M. 1949. "A Theory of Cooperation and Competition." *Human Relations* 2 (2): 129–152.

Dewey, J. 1899/1943. *The School and Society*. Chicago: University of Chicago.

Gillies, R. 2000. "The Maintenance of Cooperative and Helping Behaviour in Cooperative Groups." *British Journal of Educational Psychology* 70 (1): 97–111.

Gillies, R. 2002. "The Residual Effects of Cooperative Learning Experiences: A Two-Year Follow-Up." *The Journal of Educational Research* 96 (1): 15–22.

Gillies, R. 2004. "The Effects of Communication Training on Teachers' and Students' Verbal Behaviours During Cooperative Learning." *International Journal of Educational Research* 41 (3): 257–279.

Gillies, R. 2006. "Teachers' and Students' Verbal Behaviours During Cooperative and Small Group Learning." *British Journal of Educational Psychology* 76 (2): 271–287.

Gillies, R. M., and M. Boyle. 2008. "Teachers' Discourse During Cooperative Learning and Their Perceptions of this Pedagogical Practice." *Teacher and Teacher Education* 24 (5): 1333–1348.

Gillies, R. M., and M. Boyle. 2011. "Teachers' Reflections of Cooperative Learning (CL): A Two-Year Follow-Up." *Teaching Education* 22 (1): 63–78.

Gillies, R. M., and M. Haynes. 2011. "Increasing Explanatory Behaviour, Problem-Solving, and Reasoning with Classes Using Cooperative Group Work." *Instructional Science* 39 (3): 349–366.

Gillies, R., and A. Khan. 2009. "Promoting Reasoned Argumentation, Problem Solving and Learning During Small-Group Work." *Cambridge Journal of Education* 39 (1): 7–27.

Goldenberg, C. 1991. "Instructional Conversations and their Classroom Application." NCRCDSLL Educational Practice Reports, Center for Research on Education, Diversity and Excellence, epr2, CA: UC Berkeley.

Hammerberg, D. 2004. "Comprehension Instruction in Socioculturally Diverse Classrooms: A Review of What We Know." *The Reading Teacher* 57 (7): 648–659.

Hedegaard, M. 2003. "Cultural Minority Children's Learning within Culturally-Sensitive Classroom Teaching." *Pedagogy, Culture & Society* 11 (1): 133–152.

Hmelo-Silver, C., R. G. Duncan, and C. Clark. 2007. "Scaffolding and Achievement in Problem-Based and Inquiry Learning: A Response to Kirschner, Sweller, and Clark (2006)." *Educational Psychologist* 42 (2): 99–107.

Jimma, T., and R. Gillies. n.d. "Nurturing Cooperative Learning Pedagogies in Higher Education Classrooms: Evidence of Instructional Reform and Potential Challenges." Unpublished paper, Australia: University of Queensland.

Johnson, D. W., and R. T. Johnson. 2009. "An Educational Psychology Success Story: Social Interdependence Theory and Cooperative Learning." *Educational Researcher* 38 (5): 365–379.

Johnson, D. W., Roger T. Johnson, and Edythe Holubec. 1998. *Cooperation in the Classroom*. Boston: Allyn and Bacon.

Kagan, S., and M. Kagan. 2009. *Cooperative Learning*. San Clemente, CA: Kagan.

Kanu, Y. 2007. "Increasing School Success Among Aboriginal Students: Culturally Responsive Curriculum or Macrostructural Variables Affecting Schooling?" *Diaspora, Indigenous, and Minority Education: Studies of Migration, Integration, Equity, and Cultural Survival* 1 (1): 21–41.

Koutselini, M. 2008/2009. "Teacher Misconceptions and Understanding of Cooperative Learning: An Intervention Study." *Journal of Classroom Interaction* 43 (2): 34–44.

LEARNING TO LEARN TOGETHER

Lambert, J., and V. Mitrani. 2013. "Building Relationships Through Conversations." *Tools for Learning Schools* 16 (2): 1–3.

Lewin, K. 1947. "Frontiers in Group Dynamics: Concepts, Method, and Reality in Social Science, Social Equilibria, and Social Change." *Human Relations* 1 (1): 5–41.

Lotan, R. A. 2003. "Group-Worthy Tasks." *Educational Leadership* 6 (6): 72–75.

Magos, K., and G. Simopoulos. 2009. "Do You Know Naomi? Researching the Intercultural Competence of Teachers Who Teach Greek as a Second Language in Immigrant Classes." *Intercultural Education* 20 (3): 255–265.

Mushi, S. 2004. "Multicultural Competencies in Teaching: A Typology of Classroom Activities." *Intercultural Education* 15 (6): 179–194.

O'Bryan, B. 1999. "The Development of One Teacher's Skills at Instructional Conversation." *Reading Horizons* 39 (4): 257–277.

Ogbu, J. 1992. "Understanding Cultural Diversity and Learning." *Educational Researcher* 21 (8): 5–14.

Portera, A. 2008. "Intercultural Education in Europe: Epistemological and Semantic Aspects." *Intercultural Education* 19 (6): 481–491.

Rapport, S. 2004. Unpublished doctoral dissertation.

Saunders, W., and C. Goldenberg. 2005. "The Contribution of Settings to School Improvement and School Change: A Case Study." In *Culture and Context in Human Behavior Change: Theory, Research, and Applications*, edited by Clifford R. O'Donnell and Lois Yamauchi, 127–150. New York, NY: Peter Lang.

Schmuck, R. 2010. Keynote Address at the IASCE Conference. Brisbane, Australia.

Schmuck, R., and P. Schmuck. 2001. *Group Processes in the Classroom*. 8th ed. Boston: McGraw Hill.

Sharan, S., Y. Sharan, and I. Tan. 2013. "The Group Investigation Approach to Cooperative Learning." In *The International Handbook of Collaborative Learning*, edited by Clark Chinn, Cindy Hmelo-Silver, Angela O'Donnell, and Carol Chan, 351–369. London: Taylor and Francis.

Sharan, Y. 2010. "Cooperative Learning for Academic and Social Gains; Valued Pedagogy, Problematic Practice." *European Journal of Education* 45 (2): 300–313.

Sharan, Y. 2012a. "From the Journals, to the Field and Back." *IASCE Newsletter* 31 (1): 15–16.

Sharan, Y. 2012b. "What We can Learn from the History of Cooperative Learning." In *Perspektiver pa Cooperative Learning*, edited by Annette Hildebrand Jensen, 43–46. Denmark: Dafolo.

Sharan, Y., and S. Sharan. 1992. *Expanding Cooperative Learning Through Group Investigation*. New York, NY: Teachers College Press.

Sigel, I. and R. Cocking. 1977. *Cognitive Development from Childhood to Adolescence: A Constructionist Point of View*. New York, NY: Holt, Rinehart and Winston.

Slavin, R. E. 1999. "Student Teams-Achievement Divisions." In *Handbook of Cooperative Learning*, edited by Shlomo Sharan, 3–19. Westport, CT: Preager.

Slavin, R. E. 2010. "Instruction Based on Cooperative Learning." In *Handbook of Research on Learning and Instruction*, edited by Richard E. Mayer, 344–360. London: Taylor and Francis.

Slavin, R. E., and Nancy A. Madden, eds. 2009. *Two Million Children: Success for All*. Thousand Oaks, CA: Corwin.

Sleeter, C. E. 2012. "Confronting the Marginalization of Culturally Responsive Pedagogy." *Urban Education* 47 (3): 562–584.

Tharp, R. G., and R. Gallimore. 1988. *Rousing Minds to Life: Teaching, Learning and Schooling in Social Context*. Cambridge, UK: Cambridge University.

Tharp, R. and R. Gallimore. 1991. "The Instructional Conversation: Teaching and Learning in Social Activity (Research Report 2)." Santa Cruz, CA: The National Center for Research on Cultural Diversity and Second Language Learning.

Tharp, R. G., and L. A. Yamauchi. 1994. "Effective Instructional Conversation in Native American Classrooms." NCRCDSLL Educational Practice Reports. Berkeley, CA: Center for Research on Education, Diversity and Excellence.

Thelen, H. 1981. *The Classroom Society*. London: Croom Helm.

Vygotsky, L. 1978. *Mind in Society: The Development of Higher Psychological Processes*. Cambridge, MA: Harvard University.

Walters, L. M., B. Garii, and T. Walters. 2009. "Learning Globally, Teaching Locally: Incorporating International Exchange and Intercultural Learning into Pre-Service Teacher Training." *Intercultural Education* 20 (1): S151–S158.

Watson, J. 2001. "Social Constructivism in the Classroom." *Support for Learning* 16 (3): 140–147.

Index

Note: **Boldface** page numbers refer to figures and tables.

Aboriginal cultural knowledge 82
artwork 44
Ashton-Warner, Sylvia 80

Bologna teachers 30–3

CI model *see* Complex Instruction model
CL *see* cooperative learning
classroom intervention, cooperative learning **54,** 54–6, **55**
co-constructed chart: for cooperation 65; for writing 65
coding categories 57
cognitive dimension, in-depth qualitative analysis 57
cognitive elaboration perspectives, for cooperative learning 7
cognitive perspectives, for cooperative learning 6
Cohen, Elizabeth 26–7, 29
Cohen's status theory 29, 30
collaborative learning 51
collaborative writing 54
Comenius-funded partnership 37–8
Complex Instruction (CI) model 26, 27, 85; status problem strategies in planning activities 29–30
cooperative dimension, in-depth qualitative analysis 57
cooperative groups, status problem and participation in 26–7
cooperative learning (CL) 1, 26, 51, 66–7; *see also* meaningful learning; benefits of 52–3; case study 69–75; classroom intervention **54,** 54–6, **55**; classroom, meaningful learning in 86–8; cognitive elaboration perspectives 7; cognitive perspectives 6; data treatment and analyses 56–8; developmental perspectives 6–7; effects on learning, model of 2–3, **3**; Group

Investigation in 43; implementation of 67–9; with integrated cooperative skills training into writing tasks 54; meaningful learning creation 83–4; motivational perspectives 3–4; motivationalist perspective 2; peer interactions 52; perspectives on xiii; reconciling perspectives 8–9; research questions 54; results and discussion 58; sample and data collection 56; social cohesion perspective 5–6; sociological approach to 85; structuring group interactions 7–8; theoretical background 52–3; theoretical perspectives on 1–3, **3**; theories and application 84–6; use of 67, 73–4
cooperative skills training: second cooperative learning intervention in writing 54, **55**; theoretical background 53
co-teaching cooperative lessons 68

data collection methods, SPRinG project 14
Deutsch, Morton 84, 85
developmental perspectives, for cooperative learning 6–7
Dewey, John 84
dynamics potentially favouring learning (FL) 60–1, **61**
dynamics potentially not favouring learning (NFL) 60–1, **61**

Education Action Zone (EAZ) 70
educational systems, pedagogical approaches in 51
English language 38
environmental studies 36
Expectation States Theory 27

Finding Out/Descubrimiento programme 5

GI *see* Group Investigation
global quantitative analysis, cooperative learning 57
Group Investigation (GI) 84; in cooperative learning 43

INDEX

group work 20–1, 44; in Storyline 37; use in second language education 40
group-worthy task 88

IC *see* instructional conversations
in-depth qualitative analysis, cooperative learning 57
instructional conversations (IC) 80–1
interactive dynamics: exploratory typology of 60–1, **61**; types of 61
International Association for the Study of Cooperation in Education 67
international Storyline conference 38
Italy, educational debate 33

Key Stage 2 (KS2) 12, 23

language learners 38–41; classroom, Storyline approach impact on 41–4; negative self-image as 39
learning: constructivist and social constructivist approaches 37; cooperative Se coperative learning (CL)
learning communities, sustain in 69
Learning Together 54, 59, 85; principles of 52, 55
Lewin, Kurt 84
Likert scale 46
Lisbon Strategy, requirements of 26
literacy patterns 82

Making a Statement (MAST) project 13, xv; case studies 16–18; deliberate strategies involving peer interaction 19–20; methods 14–15; peer interaction avoided/discouraged 17; social isolation 16–17; social skills interventions 18; studies 13; systematic observation data 15–16, **16**; TA proximity restricting opportunities with peers 17–18
MAST project *see* Making a Statement project
meaningful learning 79, 80; in co-operative learning classroom 86–8; cooperative learning creation of 83–4; in multicultural classroom 81–3
motivational perspectives, for cooperative learning 3–4
motivationalist perspective, cooperative learning 2
multicultural classroom, meaningful learning in 81–3

National College for School Leadership (NCSL) 70
networked learning community (NLC) 69, 70; schools in 70
non-Aboriginal students, benefit to 82–3

On-the-Spot (OTS) Observation Categories 57

pair work 40
Paired Writing 54
peer learning 51
PLCs *see* professional learning communities
positive interdependence 66
pre-task modelling 40
professional learning communities (PLCs) 69, xvii–xviii
pupil pairs: first-level analysis 58, **58, 59**; during teamwork, global functioning of 58–9; in teamwork, interactive processes within functioning of 60

reconciling perspectives, for cooperative learning 8–9
recurrent time mode 28

SEAL *see* Social and Emotional Aspects of Learning
second language education, use of group work in 40
self-directed learning process 68
semi-structured interviews 71
SEN *see* Special Education Needs
Sharan, Yael xviii
Sharans' Group Investigation method 5, 6
shared narrative 41
Slavin, Robert xiv–xv
Social and Emotional Aspects of Learning (SEAL) 18
social behaviour, characteristics of 60
social cohesion perspective, for cooperative learning 2, 5–6
social dimension, in-depth qualitative analysis 57
social interdependence theory 2, 67–8
social isolation, MAST project 16–17
Social Pedagogic Research into Group Work (SPRinG) project 12, 13, 67; challenges identified in 20–2; control and 'holding firm' 20–2; data collection methods 14; findings from 18–19; school leadership and time 20; studies 13
social skills interventions, MAST project 18
social/positive interdependence 84–5
sociocultural theory 42
Special Education Needs (SEN) 13, 23; systematic observation data for pupils with 15, **16**; training in support of child with 19
SPRinG Lite 22–3
SPRinG project *see* Social Pedagogic Research into Group Work project
STAD *see* Student Teams-Achievement Divisions
statistical analysis: cooperative learning 57–8; crosstabs for interactive dynamics and writing tasks evolution 65
status problem: assigning competence to low-status students 30–2; definition 26;

INDEX

evaluation challenge 32; feedback 30–1; and participation in cooperative groups 26–7; research context and methodology 28; strategies in planning CI activities 29–30; teachers and goal of equity 32–3; teachers' perception of 28–9

Storyline approach: characteristic feature of 37; constructivist and social constructivist approaches 37; findings and discussion **44, 44–7, 45**; impact on young language learner classroom 41–4; key questions 42–3; and language developments 46; origination of 36; role of teacher in 37; task-based learning and teaching 41; young language learners 38–41

Structural Approach 85–6

Student Teams-Achievement Divisions (STAD) 4, 85, 86

Success for All literacy programme 71

TAs *see* teaching assistants

task-based learning and teaching (TBLT) 39, 41

Teacher (Sylvia) 80

teachers: and goal of equity 32–3; perception of status problem 28–9; role in Storyline approach 37

teaching assistants (TAs) 13; proximity restricting opportunities with peers 17–18

'Teaching Learning and Research Programme' xiii

teamwork: global functioning of pupil pairs during **58,** 58–9, **59**; interactive processes within functioning of pupil pairs in 60

traditional classroom organisation, motivationalist critique of 3–4

writing: co-constructed chart for 65; theoretical background 53–4; tool for 56

writing tasks (WT): cooperative learning with integrated cooperative skills training into 54; modes of evolution of 61

young language learners 38–41; classroom, Storyline approach impact on 41–4; negative self-image as 39

Zone of Proximal Development (ZPD) 40